INSIDE BASKETBALL

INSIDE
BASKETBALL

From the Playgrounds to the NBA

MIKE DECOURCY

MetroBooks

An Imprint of Friedman/Fairfax Publishers

© 1996 by Michael Friedman Publishing Group, Inc.

Library of Congress Cataloging-in-Publication data available upon request.

ISBN 1-56799-384-2

Editor: Stephen Slaybaugh
Art Director: Lynne Yeamans
Designer: Smay Vision
Photography Editor: Samantha Larrance

Color separations by Bright Arts Graphics (S) Pte Ltd
Printed in China by Leefung-Asco Printers Ltd.

For bulk purchases and special sales, please contact:
Friedman / Fairfax Publishers
Attention: Sales Department
15 West 26th Street
New York, NY 10010
212/685-6610 FAX 212/685-1307

Visit the Friedman/Fairfax Website:
http://www.webcom.com/friedman

Dedication

To Pat, who introduced me to basketball; Deac, who helped me learn to love the game; and, most of all, Debbie, who loves me in spite of it.

Acknowledgments

This being my first book, I could not have come close to completing the project without the assistance of a number of capable people. Special thanks to my editor, Steve Slaybaugh; to colleagues Steve Hubbard, Tom Yantz, Adrian Wojarnowski, Andy Katz, Dave Krieger, Todd Jones, David Williams, Ron Higgins, Ken Davis, and Rick Bonnell; to Robin Deutsch of the Naismith Memorial Basketball Hall of Fame; to Anfernee Hardaway of the Orlando Magic, Jimmy Jackson of the Dallas Mavericks, and all the players and coaches who were such willing interview subjects; and Dick Vitale, who is as classy as he is verbose. I'd also like to express my gratitude to my bosses at *The Commercial Appeal*, who gave me the freedom necessary to do the work, notably executive sports editor John Stamm. Thanks to Michael Leonardi for providing energetic research assistance. And finally I'd like to thank my wife, Debbie, who was at once the best secretary, copyreader, and friend I could hope for.

CONTENTS

For Love or Money

I t is a steamy July day, and Jimmy Jackson of the Dallas Mavericks is a wealthy young man with time on his hands. He could be off in the mountains or at the shore, lounging in a plush condominium or playing golf on a challenging course. Instead, he is sitting at a summer camp for high school kids, watching intently as they play, enjoying the sport that has become his life.

This is the essence of basketball, the aspect of the game that lifts it above other sports. There is no off-season, because no one really wants a break. People take holidays from their work, not from their passion. "If they weren't paying what they were paying," says Los Angeles Lakers forward Cedric Ceballos, "and there was an ability for me to play basketball anywhere whatsoever—rec ball, adult league, anything—I would play and still have the same love for it." Other professional athletes occasionally say they would play their game for free, but it seems only basketball players live up to that promise.

In the summer at the University of Pittsburgh, you might find former Panthers Charles Smith of the San Antonio Spurs or Eric Mobley of the Vancouver Grizzlies sharing the court with players still

on the Pitt team. Jackson heads back to Columbus, Ohio, where he played at Ohio State, and joins in pickup games and summer leagues with the OSU players. At the University of Memphis, NBA all-star Anfernee Hardaway of the Orlando Magic plays pickup ball with the current Tigers and with Phoenix Suns guard Elliot Perry and Bucks guard Todd Day. All-star forward Scottie Pippen of the Chicago Bulls plays in a charity game and finds he can still surprise and delight himself—and thousands of fans—by tossing the ball off the backboard on a fast break and slamming it through the goal.

How often will you find a dozen big-league baseball players mixing with some college and high school kids for an informal game of hardball? It doesn't happen. The sticks most hockey players swing in the summer are golf clubs. Football players spend their off-season time lifting weights to grow their muscles.

"It's tough for football players in the off-season to get a good game going," Jackson says. "It's easy for a basketball player to get a game, because it's played everywhere."

We are asked to believe that basketball is the game of the inner city, where games are played on asphalt playgrounds squeezed between high-rise buildings, the goals have chain-link nets or no nets at all, and the greatest value is placed on the player who can beat his man to the goal and elevate above

FAR LEFT: Los Angeles Lakers guard Nick Van Exel thrives on the late-game pressure situations basketball tends to create more often than other sports. If there is a game on the line, Van Exel wants the decisive shot to come from his hand. LEFT: Taller than most of his childhood teammates, Jimmy Jackson, now of the Dallas Mavericks, developed his ballhandling and shooting skills at an early age, which made him ready to play as a shooting guard when he arrived in the NBA.

ABOVE: All-time great Magic Johnson of the Los Angeles Lakers got the chance to introduce himself to the new breed of basketball stars, such as Golden State forward Joe Smith, on the night he came back to the NBA after four seasons of retirement. OPPOSITE: Chicago Bulls forward Dennis Rodman tries to block his former teammate and San Antonio Spur David Robinson's shot as new teammates Michael Jordan and Scottie Pippen wait for the rebound. Trading for Rodman helped Chicago compile the greatest regular season in NBA history.

the rim for a devastating dunk. And yet the sport has been adopted at least as vigorously by the shirtless Ohio teenagers populating a water park's cement court on a mid-summer afternoon, bothered no more by the ninety-degree temperatures than by the distractions of the nearby wave pool and its attendant bikinis.

As surely as there are cornstalks growing tall on nearly every corner in Iowa, there are basketball goals sprouting like weeds in America's driveways and parking lots, from telephone poles and barn walls. The number of people in the U.S. who consider themselves basketball players has grown by a third since 1987, from 35.7 million to 47.3 million, and those who play regularly have increased by more than 60 percent. Basketball is the favorite sport of 36 percent more Americans now than only a

decade ago. The game can be played five-on-five, three-on-three, one-on-one or, most blessedly, one-on-none, the player needing only a ball and a basket and the challenge of improving his skills.

"All the economic barriers are broken down. You don't even need a net," says coach John Calipari, who energized the program at the University of Massachusetts. "It's a game that parallels life's challenges in that you are able to achieve certain things on your own, but the bulk of what happens is with the team. The bottom line is to mesh your skills with the five to eight other people."

When NBA great Magic Johnson was not playing with the Los Angeles Lakers, he was often a spectator at college games like the NCAA Final Four. After retiring, he played for the U.S. Dream Team in the 1992 Barcelona Olympics and later formed a team of semi professional players and took them on international tours. As part of the Lakers' ownership group, he talked periodically of making a comeback. In 1996 he rejoined the team halfway through the season, bringing anticipation and excitement to the game, before calling it quits again at the end of the season. At the NBA's annual predraft tryout camp for college players, you will find a virtual Hall of Fame of retired greats in the stands: Jerry West, Larry Bird, Kevin McHale, Elgin Baylor, Willis Reed. They attend the camp to scout for various professional teams. Years after their playing careers ended, they cannot escape the game's allure.

What these men achieved has made them no more devoted to the game than Josh Pastner, a teenager from suburban Houston who longs one day to become a college coach. He regularly competes against players who continue to dream of careers in the NBA, but he grew out of that a while back, and now spends nearly as much time watching his contemporaries play as working on his own skills. He tips off scouting services and colleges on the identities of talented, unknown players. He rarely wanders far from a basketball court.

"Whenever I have the ball, I always feel comfortable," Pastner says. "No matter what happens, as long as I have basketball, I feel comfortable. I think that's what draws people to the game: they feel comfortable. It's like second nature. They've been doing it all their lives, they practice every day, and the ball just becomes part of their hand. They feel they have power in the game."

Pastner may have limited gifts as a player, but he has learned the same lesson as Jackson, one of the world's greatest players.

"Watching the game, being around it, loving to play the game, wanting to be as good as I could be—it's an appreciation I acquired more than anything else," Jimmy Jackson says. "If you want to be as good as you can, you're always around the game. That's during the season, preseason, off-season, whatever. I like to play. I like to watch. I like to be around it. This is the game I love."

CHAPTER ONE

Origins

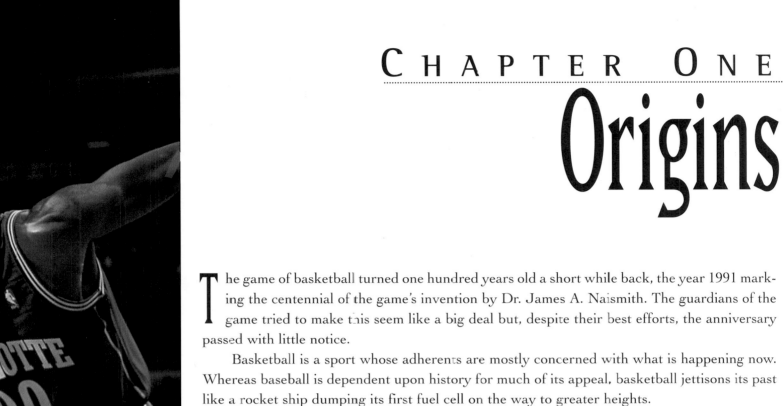

T he game of basketball turned one hundred years old a short while back, the year 1991 marking the centennial of the game's invention by Dr. James A. Naismith. The guardians of the game tried to make this seem like a big deal but, despite their best efforts, the anniversary passed with little notice.

Basketball is a sport whose adherents are mostly concerned with what is happening now. Whereas baseball is dependent upon history for much of its appeal, basketball jettisons its past like a rocket ship dumping its first fuel cell on the way to greater heights.

If not for Naismith, however, Michael Jordan would probably have been a center fielder and Karl Malone a defensive end. If not for Hank Luisetti, there might be no compelling reason to watch the sport on television. And if not for George Mikan, there might not be a National Basketball Association.

It was hardly inevitable that the game of basketball should be invented. There was a little luck involved, a great deal of inspiration, and, as with most inventions, a need to be filled.

Naismith was an instructor at the Springfield, Massachusetts YMCA college in the winter of 1891, a time when there was baseball to occupy the spring and summer, football for the autumn, but nothing to keep physical education students busy in the winter other than calisthenics. One such class, consisting largely of students in their late twenties, became difficult for the Springfield faculty to handle. Naismith, challenged by school president Dr. Luther Gulick to restore order in the class, set out to ease the students' boredom.

The first several experiments at developing an indoor game failed, as Naismith attempted to squeeze soccer and lacrosse into his gym. He thought about football, but knew it was too rough for the hard wooden floors. He decided he needed to invent an entirely new game. He figured that his new game would have to include a ball, since most popular team sports did, and that running with the ball would have to be outlawed in order to eliminate the roughness that went with football and rugby.

He chose to have the players pass the ball—originally a regulation soccer ball—toward a target, and placed that target above their heads in order to prevent defensive players from ganging up on the one with the ball. He asked the school custodian for a couple of eighteen-inch (46cm) boxes to serve as the goals, but none were available. Naismith was offered peach baskets instead. They were nailed to a ledge in the gymnasium, which happened to be ten feet (3m) above the floor.

FAR LEFT: With the ball in Michael Jordan's control, Chicago teammate Bill Wennington and Charlotte center Robert Parish are mere spectators. Because of his unmatched body control and competitiveness, Jordan is widely acknowledged as the best basketball player ever. ABOVE: In its initial incarnation, basketball was played using peach baskets and a soccer ball. LEFT: Although he invented what became one of the world's most popular sports, Dr. James A. Naismith believed more strongly in the healthful benefits of exercise than in the value of competition.

When George Mikan entered the NBA after leaving DePaul University, he was such a gate attraction the marquee at Madison Square Garden once read: "George Mikan vs. the Knicks."

Basketball pioneer Dr. Walter Meanwell meant so much to the University of Wisconsin, the school had a life-sized bronze plaque dedicated in his honor.

Naismith wrote out the original thirteen rules of basketball and tacked them to the gymnasium wall. Several of these rules are still in force today: no personal fouls, no traveling with the ball, no goaltending, and five seconds to inbound the ball after a change of possession. In just two weeks, he had invented a game that would one day captivate the world.

Basketball rapidly spread as a winter diversion, gaining popularity in varied regions of the country. The original version featured nine-man teams, but a Springfield faculty member named Amos Alonzo Stagg—who became a football coach and won more gridiron games than any other— came up with the idea to have five on a side in 1892. On January 16, 1896, two teams representing the University of Chicago and the University of Iowa played an intercollegiate game using five-men lineups. However, the Iowa team was filled with ringers (ineligible players) from the local YMCA; for this reason, the Yale-Penn meeting on March 20, 1897, is generally regarded as the first college basketball game.

The game did not catch on with spectators at first, largely because it was bound by techniques and technicalities that deadened its appeal. Until 1937, rules required that a jump ball at center court follow every field goal made. Tall players were allowed to remain stationary beneath the goal and wait to catch the ball, until the 3-second lane was introduced in 1935. There was no 10-second line until the 1930s, which meant there was no incentive to advance the ball quickly toward the basket.

Players tended to stand in place and pass the ball until one of them had room to fire a two-handed shot. Dr. Walter Meanwell, who coached from 1911 to 1933 at the University of Wisconsin, bucked the trend of static offenses to introduce the fast break, screens for shooters, and offensive motion. But conservative coaches fought the development of the one-handed shot, which did not require as much time or room to launch as the conventional set shot, and thus opened the possibility of faster-paced, higher-scoring games.

Just how slowly did basketball develop? Metal rims and nets made of cord were introduced quickly, but it took nearly two decades, until 1906, for somebody to figure out that the bottom could be cut from the net, allowing the ball to pass through after a goal so that play could continue.

The person who did the most to energize basketball and open the possibilities of offensive excitement was Hank Luisetti, a six-foot-two-inch (187cm) guard for Stanford University who averaged more than 20 points per game at a time when that was a terrific scoring average for an entire team. He could dribble behind his back and was known for his hang time when he drove to the basket, but his specialty was a one-handed shot. Some successful eastern coaches, whose strategies relied on the sta-

bility of the two-handed shot, called Luisetti's one-hander a threat to the foundations of the game.

Luisetti made his Madison Square Garden debut on December 30, 1936, scoring 15 points in a 45–32 Stanford victory over Long Island University that broke LIU's 43-game winning streak. That was enough to convince many doubters the game could be played differently, better. The *New York Times* wrote that he "could do nothing wrong. Some of his shots would have been deemed foolhardy if attempted by any other player, but with Luisetti doing the heaving, these were accepted by the crowd as a matter of course." He went on to score 50 points in one game, a 92–27 victory against Duquesne in 1938.

A game that had been stagnant for nearly fifty years began to change rapidly, and that is one element of the game that has remained constant in the more than fifty years since: change. The 3-second lane has grown wider, play has become more physical, and behind-the-back passes that were once considered hot-dogging are now routine. And players have grown taller.

When six-foot-ten-inch (208cm) George Mikan began to play for DePaul University in the early 1940s, his one true rival among big men was seven-foot-tall (213cm) Bob Kurland of Oklahoma A&M (now Oklahoma State). The two of them introduced the concept of the dominant big man to the game. Mikan averaged 40 points per game in leading DePaul to the National Invitation Tournament title in 1945, while Kurland lifted Oklahoma A&M to the NCAA Championship.

Kurland's contributions to the game tend to be forgotten because he accepted a job with Phillips Petroleum after graduation and played in industrial leagues. Mikan, by contrast, accepted a $5,000 offer to play professional basketball, and his presence was the gate attraction that sold the NBA in its early days.

Naismith lived long enough to see the game become a success, but not the phenomenon it became later. He moved to the University of Kansas and became director of the Phys. Ed. department and head basketball coach. There, he worked with a man named Forrest "Phog" Allen, who would become coach at Kansas and work with a player named Dean Smith, who would become coach at North Carolina and work with a player named Michael Jordan.

Allen was perhaps the first of the game's great coaches, winning 590 games at Kansas and the 1952 NCAA Championship, as well as the 1952 Olympic gold medal as coach of the U.S. team. He loved to expound theories of the game, and, while coaching under him, was telling Naismith about some of his ideas when Naismith stopped him and said, "You don't coach this game, Forrest, you just play it."

Which perhaps explains why James A. Naismith is the only basketball coach in Kansas history to compile a losing record.

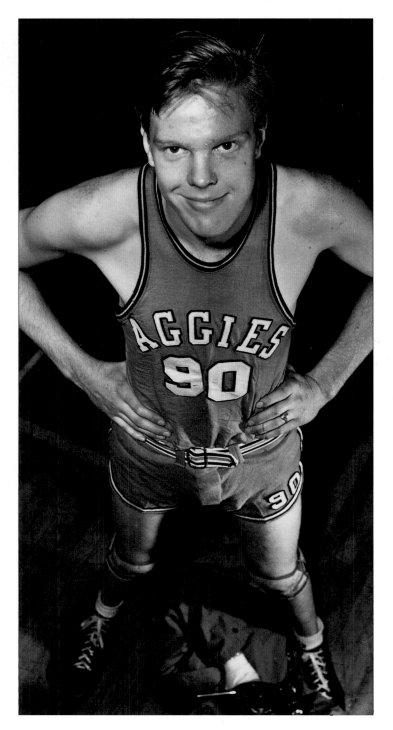

Standing just under seven feet (213cm), Bob Kurland found it so easy to swat shots away from the basket that he caused the NCAA to institute the goaltending rule.

CONFERENCE CLASHES

As he was getting close to the end of his college basketball career, Michigan State guard Shawn Respert couldn't wait for the NCAA Tournament to begin. He had simply had enough of the game as it is played in the Big Ten Conference.

Of course, he felt that way in the second half of all four seasons he played with the Spartans. After they'd played all the Big Ten opponents once, he knew the games would get uglier the second time around. "It's so much tougher in the second half of the Big Ten season, because teams know what your strategies are, what you do offensively and defensively," says Respert, now with the Milwaukee Bucks.

"Usually, when you get into the tournament, you're facing somebody new, and they have no idea what you're going to do and you have no idea what they do. It's not that much pressure mentally."

Teams in the Big Ten get off easier than those in other conferences because that league does not play a postseason tournament to decide its champion. In the Big Eight Conference, Kansas might play Oklahoma State three times in one season, the same for Georgetown and Syracuse in the Big East. This gives players and coaches on each side the chance to learn every nuance of the other team's style. If a guy likes to drive the right side, he will no doubt find a defender blocking his path every time. If a team doesn't operate well against a full-court pressure defense, it is likely to encounter that tactic through the course of the game. This is a classic case of paralysis by analysis.

"You become familiar by playing them, and you tend to watch all the conference games on television," says Charlie Spoonhour, the coach at Saint Louis University. "And it's just the idea that people in conferences, everybody treats those games special. Even though you want to win every game you play, the conference games take on added significance. You never have an easy conference game on the road. I've never seen such a thing."

Of the 302 teams that play basketball in the NCAA's Division I, fewer than ten do not belong to a conference. Members play for league championships that automatically place them into the NCAA Tournament. A team that begins a season with some unexpected losses can use the conference schedule to erase that disappointment.

There is more pride at stake when teams in the same conference play, because they know they'll be back together soon, sharing the same court. Conference teams often develop intense rivalries. Some are based on sustained excellence in two programs, which keeps them fighting for the same prizes. Arizona and UCLA, for instance, have dominated the Pacific-10 Conference for the past decade, and their games have become highly competitive. Some rivalries develop on geography alone, such as Alabama and Auburn in the Southeastern Conference. The best rivalries involve some combination of those factors, such as that between North Carolina and Duke in the Atlantic Coast Conference. They are just miles apart in eastern Carolina's Research Triangle area. Between them, they have won five NCAA championships and made twenty-three Final Four appearances. There are numbers, though, that may be even more important: Duke has won eleven ACC titles, North Carolina twenty-two. North Carolina holds a 116–78 all-time series lead.

The most curious aspect of conference competition, though, is that it exists not only within the leagues, but also between them. After dominating the Final Four in the late 1980s, the Big East didn't get one team that far in the next six years. Rivals delighted in the former bully's sudden struggles. At the 1994 Final Four in the Charlotte Coliseum, fans from Florida and Arkansas joined together in a chant of "S-E-C" to celebrate their league's unexpected success that season.

When six teams from the Big Ten were gone after the second round of the 1995 NCAA Tournament, their players and coaches fielded as many questions about their league's failures as their individual disappointments. Fans of all the major conferences—including the ACC, Big East, and Conference USA, the newest league—want to believe their teams play the best basketball.

"You identify yourself by what you do in your conference," says Tennessee coach Kevin O'Neill, who won a title in the defunct Great Midwest Conference when he was coach at Marquette University. "You should recruit to win your conference and play to win it. And what you should do is go from there and hope your conference does well. I'm one of those people who always pulls for people in my league, unless they're against me."

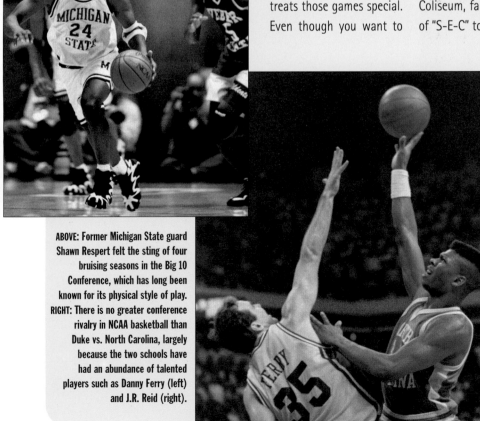

ABOVE: Former Michigan State guard Shawn Respert felt the sting of four bruising seasons in the Big 10 Conference, which has long been known for its physical style of play.
RIGHT: There is no greater conference rivalry in NCAA basketball than Duke vs. North Carolina, largely because the two schools have had an abundance of talented players such as Danny Ferry (left) and J.R. Reid (right).

Standing only five feet eleven inches (180cm), UCLA guard Tyus Edney had no trouble making big plays against bigger players like Louisville's six-foot-four-inch (193cm) Tick Rogers.

The NCAA

Tyus Edney glanced at the scoreboard, and it was all bad news. His UCLA Bruins were trailing Missouri by a point in the second round of the 1995 NCAA Tournament, and fewer than 4 seconds remained in the game. He looked downcourt and saw five opponents ready to stop him and spoil the top-ranked Bruins' dream of returning UCLA to college basketball dominance.

What happened from that moment is almost a blur, because Edney made his miracle happen so quickly. He dribbled around and through four of the Tigers, stopped eight feet (2.44m) from the basket, and jumped into the air, hanging there long enough to elude the last of his opponents and sling the ball off the backboard and into the net. UCLA won by a point. Four games later, the Bruins claimed the NCAA Championship.

"[There's] a fine line between winning and losing," says UCLA coach Jim Harrick. "I think if you ask any coach who's won a national championship, he'll say, 'Some way you have to get lucky.' Tyus Edney is a great player who made a great play, but…I think we were lucky at that particular moment on that particular play."

Moments such as that one happen almost routinely in college basketball. On the way to its 1992 championship, Duke defeated Kentucky in the East Regional final when forward Grant Hill threw a seventy-five-foot pass to center Christian Laettner, who turned, dribbled, and fired a seventeen-foot jumper that slammed through the goal. All this in 2.1 seconds. North Carolina won in 1993 because Michigan, down 1 point in the final seconds, called a timeout without having one available, which is a technical foul.

In the 1981 tournament, which may have changed forever the way college basketball is perceived, fans watching on television saw three teams win on last-second shots in one afternoon: St. Joseph's upset number-one DePaul, 49-48; Kansas State shot down highly ranked Oregon State on a long jumper by guard Rolando Blackman; and Arkansas knocked out defending champion Louisville when guard U.S. Reed heaved a fifty-foot shot from just past midcourt. The Saturday of thrills convinced television networks they could dazzle fans by showing the conclusion of every tight early-round game.

Of the NCAA championship games since 1980, 10 weren't decided until the final minute of play. Since the tournament expanded to sixty-four teams and it became necessary to win 6 games to claim the title, no champion has made it through without at least 1 close game.

"The NCAA Tournament is the fastest-growing sporting event in the country," says CBS-TV announcer Jim Nantz, who has broadcast the event for a decade. "It is something so loved, so endearing in its pureness. There is no other sport that for one month completely captivates the sports audience like the NCAA Tournament. March is owned by college basketball."

It isn't just the tournament that makes college basketball special. The game has also grown because of its volume and variety. There are more than three hundred teams that begin the season each year with a goal of reaching the Final Four, giving fans in nearly every corner of the United States direct access to a favorite. Whereas college football generally has the same teams ranked at the top from year to year, basketball had twenty-one different programs reach the Final Four between 1986 and 1995.

College basketball has thrived because of its unique flavor, with pep bands creating a noisy atmosphere at such historic sites as the Harmon Gym at UC Berkeley and UCLA's Pauley Pavilion, and fans joining in traditional cheers such as the Hog Call at Arkansas or the "Rock, Chalk, Jayhawk" recited by Kansas fans. Duke students have made a tradition out of camping out beside Cameron Indoor Stadium to get the best seats for big games.

The college game is more cerebral than the NBA version. Zone defenses are permitted, which means there are more options to consider, and the shot clock allows teams to hold the ball for 35 seconds, probing for weaknesses in the opposing defense instead of reacting to the first opportunity. Teams must be capable of handling a variety of strategic challenges, from the full-court press to the box-and-one defense. They aren't always, which is why "upset"

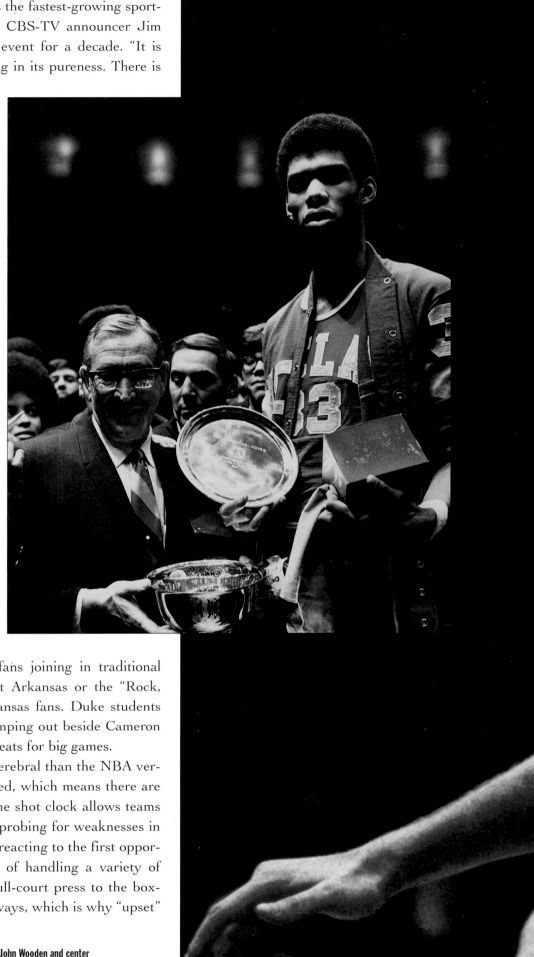

ABOVE: At the center of the UCLA dynasty were coach John Wooden and center Lew Alcindor (later known as Kareem Abdul-Jabbar) who combined to win three national championships and 88 of 90 games. RIGHT: The 1992 NCAA Tournament game between Kentucky and Duke, which Blue Devils forward Christian Laettner (right) won with a seventeen-foot (5.1m) jumper at the buzzer, is considered the greatest college game ever played.

Arkansas ended Duke's dream of winning three NCAA titles in four years when the Razorbacks claimed the 1994 championship at Charlotte Coliseum.

is one of the most common words in the language of college basketball.

"The team with the most talent doesn't always win," says Mike Deane, head coach at Marquette University. "And thank God for that."

The same teams tend to be near the top of the rankings each year. Schools like Kentucky, North Carolina, and Kansas rely on tradition, support, and successful coaches such as Rick Pitino, Dean Smith, and Roy Williams to make annual tournament appearances and collect 20-victory seasons. Those teams combined to make six Final Four trips in the first half of the 1990s.

Purdue University in West Lafayette, Indiana, however, offers an example of how a team that does not attract

the most gifted players can still achieve spectacular results. As only the third most prominent program in the state, behind Indiana and Notre Dame, Purdue usually is unable to recruit the prime high school talent. Glenn Robinson of the Milwaukee Bucks, college basketball's player of the year in 1994, is the only Purdue product in recent years who has become a star in the pros.

Coach Bob Knight's Indiana is the program of choice for many of his state's top prospects; Knight led Indiana to NCAA titles in 1976, 1981, and 1987. Michigan, which won the NCAA crown in 1989, annually loads up on marvelous athletes from Detroit and other areas of the country. And yet Purdue has won seven championships in the rugged Big Ten Conference, and has made eleven trips to

the NCAA Tournament under Gene Keady. The Boilermakers tend to adopt Keady's ferocious, combative approach to the game, and win by playing stifling defense and intelligent offense.

"I think our work ethic is a bit better than a lot of people's," Keady says. "The kids work hard at fundamentals, and they get to where they understand the game pretty well and to know if we play pretty good defense and take good shots, that will win us some games."

College teams can rise quickly by recruiting two or three talented players, which is what happened at the University of Massachusetts. When the Minutemen first hired John Calipari as their coach, they were a consistently losing program. He began bringing in talented high school athletes, and by his fourth year, UMass was regularly among the Top 25 teams.

"I know guys who are skilled players, but the biggest thing we look for is competitiveness. Is the guy a warrior?" Calipari said. "Will he compete, will he battle, does he have a burning desire to win? Then you can overcome the other scars in their game. The kid that's the great player, great shooter, great student, they don't come to UMass."

The college game has had to be resilient throughout the course of its history. No matter how many times it is buried, college basketball comes back even stronger. It survived point-shaving scandals in the 1950s and 1960s, the numbing domination of the game by UCLA in the 1960s and 1970s, and the explosion of the NBA's popularity in the 1980s.

In the 1990s, the challenge to college ball has been the exodus of star players to the professional ranks after short stays in college. Kenny Anderson, Chris Webber, Joe Smith, Anfernee Hardaway, Jason Kidd: each of them played only two seasons before entering the NBA draft. Players came to view college as a two-year stop on the way to the pros.

College basketball remains as popular as ever, creating new stars each year to replace the ones who depart. More of its games are televised by national networks, broadcast and cable, than any other sport. The television ratings for the Final Four are competitive with just about any major event.

Basketball began in a campus atmosphere, at the Springfield YMCA school, and that is where its popularity started to spread. By the time Yale beat Penn in

North Carolina guard Donald Williams shot his way to a Final Four MVP Award when the Tar Heels became 1993 NCAA champs.

Before his dramatic halfcourt shot to beat Louisville in the 1981 NCAA Tournament, Arkansas' U.S. Reed scored on this routine layup.

1897 in what is recognized as the first game between two sanctioned college teams using five players each, the game already was being played in various forms at colleges in Minnesota, Illinois, and Iowa. A decade later, schools were forming conferences and playing more intersectional games. Growth in the 1920s and early 1930s was limited by the tiny gyms where the games were played and by the lack of a championship tournament to increase interest nationally. A young newspaperman named Ned Irish helped take care of both. Irish became convinced of the

sport's potential when he was assigned to cover a college basketball game at a gym that seated twelve hundred spectators. He arrived after the place was already packed, so crowded he could not get through the door, so Irish climbed through a window, tearing his pants in the process. He knew the game was ready to grow.

In 1934, Irish organized a doubleheader at Madison Square Garden, at which New York University defeated Notre Dame and Westminster College of Pennsylvania beat St. John's. A crowd of more than sixteen thousand people attended. The doubleheaders remained successful for decades, and Irish went on to help develop the National Invitation Tournament in 1938. This allowed the best college teams to be brought to Madison Square Garden for a postseason competition. It also prompted the National Association of Basketball Coaches to convince the NCAA one year later to hold the first national championship. Teams from Oregon, Ohio State, Villanova, and Oklahoma were the members of the first Final Four, with Oregon winning the title over Ohio State by a 46–33 score in Evanston, Illinois.

By the late 1940s, college basketball was the most popular winter sport in America and the rage of New York City, where such teams as Long Island University, City College of New York, Manhattan, and St. John's dominated the game. As the 1950s dawned, however, three of LIU's players were charged with fixing games. The investigation uncovered evidence that players for several top schools had been paid for years to lose games or to "shave points," which is when a team attempts to win by fewer points than oddsmakers say it should.

It took three decades, the expansion of the NCAA Tournament, and the spread of cable television to put college basketball back where it had been.

The program that ruled basketball during much of that time of rebuilding was UCLA, coached by Hall of Famer John Wooden. The Bruins visited the Final Four thirteen times from 1962 through 1976, and won ten NCAA Championships between 1964 and 1975. The Bruins were led by seven-foot-two-inch (218cm) center Lew Alcindor (now Kareem Abdul-Jabbar) from 1967 to 1969 and by six-foot-eleven-inch (210cm) Bill Walton from 1972 to 1974.

"A lot of teams would lay down to UCLA just because of the name," says Jimmy Collins, a star guard on the New Mexico State team that lost to the Bruins in the 1970 NCAA semifinals. He is now an assistant coach at the University of Illinois. "The difference now is that you've got parity. If you can put a team together that can go all they way now...you've definitely worked. UCLA, they just naturally got all the top players. I think that's the major difference in developing a championship team today is that you've really got to work to do that because everyone can play. At that particular time everybody that could play went to UCLA."

When UCLA was winning championships, only conference winners and selected independents were allowed in the NCAA Tournament. After the rules were changed in 1975 to include more teams, the tournament developed the unpredictable nature that made it the country's most fascinating sporting event. From 1974 through 1982, average attendance at tournament games nearly doubled. By 1994, CBS-TV had determined that broadcast rights to the tournament were worth $1.7 billion over seven years.

The Madison Square Garden doubleheaders that featured such teams as Notre Dame and New York University (above) helped build the game that made national names of DePaul forwards Terry Cummings and Mark Aguirre (top).

"The Final Four is what you dream and play and work for every year," Jim Harrick says. "But even if you don't get that far, it doesn't mean you didn't have a great year. I judge our year more based on if our kids played up to their potential and ability. A lot of teams play better than their talent should allow them to play and get farther than anybody would give them a legitimate chance to get."

The ABA

The American Basketball Association gave the world Julius Erving, "hardship cases," the Indiana Pacers, and the three-point goal. These are among the few lasting monuments of the league's brief, dynamic existence, but those who remember the ABA remember the ball: that red, white, and blue ball that seemed to sparkle in flight. And they remember the characters.

The ABA was conceived during the late sixties, and it came to have a good deal of that period's anti-establishment attitude. The league was filled with unusual personalities, like Warren Jabali, the

six-foot-two-inch (187cm) guard for Miami and Denver whom Memphis guard Larry Finch called "the meanest man in the game." Or John Brisker, for years the leading scorer with the Pittsburgh Condors, who is believed to have fought as a mercenary in Uganda, and who was declared dead after he disappeared.

In the 1970s, as the league matured, people began to appreciate the ABA's accomplished and appealing style of basketball. "You had your animals and tough guys; that was part of the game," says Mel Daniels, a four-time all-star center with the Indiana Pacers. "Intimidation is part of professional basketball. I don't think it was what we were all about. I think what we were about was being innovative: the dunk contests, three-point contests, those types of things. We tried to make our league as glamorous, attractive, and competitive as possible.

"I think simply because we were kind of like stepchildren, it made the league play harder. It was very competi-

ABOVE: The ABA enabled Ron Boone to grow from an unknown to one of basketball's great scorers with the Utah Stars.
RIGHT: When he joined the Virginia Squires after playing in obscurity at the University of Massachusetts, few expected Julius "Dr. J" Erving to become the biggest name in basketball.

Empty seats were more the rule than the exception in the ABA, despite such great players as Denver forward Spencer Haywood.

tive. People wanted to prove they were worthy of being in the National Basketball Association, and all of a sudden it got to the point where we thought we were better. We wanted this thing to succeed, and the only way to do it was to work harder."

The ABA was founded after an ambitious group of California businessmen noticed the success of the American Football League, which forced a merger with the established National Football League after just a half-dozen years of operation.

The owners hired basketball legend George Mikan as commissioner. The unusual tri-colored ball was his suggestion, and he declared that all shots made from beyond twenty-five feet (7.62m) would be worth 3 points. The ABA signed star forward Rick Barry away from the NBA, grabbed Daniels out of college, and provided a place for the great Connie Hawkins to play; he had been banned from the NBA after being wrongly implicated in a gambling scandal.

The ill-fated league began its first season on Friday, the thirteenth of October, 1967, with the Oakland Oaks defeating the Anaheim Amigos, 134–129. The Oaks had to do it without their expected star, Barry, who was ordered

by a court to sit out one season to fulfill his contract with the NBA's San Francisco Warriors.

Hawkins thus became the unquestioned star of the new league. That first season, 1967–1968, Hawkins averaged 27 points, 14 rebounds, and 5 assists, leading Pittsburgh to the inaugural ABA title. When the following season opened, the franchise had moved to Minnesota, a clear indication of what the ABA would be about. In all, twenty-two different cities played host to ABA teams. Only once in its history did all the teams stay in the same place from one year to the next. There were negotiations for a merger with the NBA almost throughout the ABA's existence.

The ABA was a league that provided opportunities. Roger Brown and Doug Moe were victims of the same scandals as Hawkins, though they were never found guilty of any wrongdoing. Brown became a great player with the Indiana Pacers; Moe played five seasons with four different teams and went on to become an innovative coach in the ABA and NBA. Players like guard Ron Boone, an eleventh-round draft choice out of Idaho State for the NBA's Phoenix Suns, chose the ABA for the opportunity

Kentucky Colonels center Artis Gilmore was one of the few legitimate seven-footers (213cm) in the ABA. He averaged 22 points and 17 rebounds before the league folded following his fifth professional

it provided to play and improve. "I just thought my chances were better," Boone says. "I thought I was a late developer, and through the ABA I got a chance to get that playing time on the court until I turned out to be a really good player."

With seven-foot-two-inch (218cm) Artis Gilmore, gifted forward George McGinnis, and Erving joining the league, the ABA's product kept getting better, but the league was never stable except on the court. In five seasons, the Memphis franchise went through three nicknames: the Pros, the Sounds, and the Tams (which stood for Tennessee-Arkansas-Mississippi). The team also had four coaches and six owners—the league took over the team's operation twice—and went through twenty-eight

asked to suggest their ideas, with the winner receiving a television set. The name chosen was Pioneers. The problem was, the city's Point Park College already used that nickname and threatened to sue. The basketball team agreed to change its name, but didn't want to award another TV. After sifting through the entries, team officials discovered no one had suggested Condors. The bird is not yet extinct, but the team was within three years.

The league rarely followed convention. The first college player to leave school for the pros came through the ABA's door, when Spencer Haywood of the University of Detroit signed with Denver in 1969. Players were supposed to finish their careers in college before playing for pay, but Haywood was deemed a "hardship case." When center Moses Malone was coming out of high school in Petersburg, Virgina, in 1974, the owners of the Utah Stars figured he was ready for their team and offered a $3 million contract. He became the league's rookie of the year, but the Stars were out of business the following season.

"Off the court, the league wasn't that stable," Boone says, "and some teams had so many players running in and out. There was always someone there trying to get your job. I think it was a very loose league. I didn't look at it as being wild, that's for sure, but I did look at it as a league that was wide open. I think the playing style the ABA used is what you see now: the run-and-gun, the three-point shot, the strong guard/forward play because we didn't have the big men."

The final ABA championship was won by Julius Erving and the New York Nets, who beat the Denver Nuggets in 6 games. The last of those was a 112–106 Nets win on May 13, 1976. The league was dead a month later, when owners from the NBA and ABA agreed to a merger of sorts.

The ABA lives on in the form of the Pacers, the Nets (since moved to New Jersey), the Denver Nuggets, and the San Antonio Spurs, all taken into the NBA when the merger was completed; each team payed an entry fee of $3.2 million. None of the remaining ABA teams has ever reached the NBA Finals. And there is other evidence of the ABA's legacy. Like Haywood, dozens of players with college eligibility remaining enter the pro draft each year. And Erving and Malone will eventually take their place in the Hall of Fame.

"The Indiana Pacers, the New Jersey franchise, Denver, and San Antonio are monuments to hard work, that we were a viable league, that we had talent," Daniels says. "It makes the old fellas feel good about what we accomplished."

The red, white, and blue ball, which was the ball of choice for pickup games as long as the ABA endured, has disappeared. Like the wooden tennis racket and canvas sneaker, it has become a museum piece.

players in a single season. In ten seasons, there were seven commissioners, from the Hall of Fame center who oversaw its creation (Mikan) to the Hall of Fame power forward who was there at the end (Dave DeBusschere).

Along the way there were some of the oddest episodes in big-league sports. The Pittsburgh Condors came by their nickname after sponsoring a contest in which fans were

The NBA

The three initials that have made the National Basketball Association the most popular sporting association in the world are of little use to those U.S. teenagers who dream of playing for the New York Knicks or the Cleveland Cavaliers. They simply call it "The League."

The players who make it, though, don't always do a lot of dreaming or talking along the way. They do more playing, practicing, and hoping. "The ones who make it," says Milwaukee Bucks guard Shawn Respert, "are the ones who are humble and always think they have to improve."

Los Angeles Lakers guard Nick Van Exel, perhaps the most confident player in the league, never really considered the idea of a professional career until he became a star during his senior season at the University of Cincinnati. He grew up in Kenosha, Wisconsin, home to few NBA players. "My biggest dream when I was little was to play [NCAA] Division I basketball, so people could see me. I never imagined playing in the NBA because nobody from my hometown ever made it. I didn't have anybody to look up to."

NBA players are members of the most exclusive club in major team sports. Each of the twenty-nine teams carries twelve players, which means there are only 348 jobs available. The players in the NBA are considered by many to be the best athletes in the world because they must be able to run fast, jump high, be precise in their actions, and cooperate with team members. And because they're so big. The lineup that carried the Orlando Magic to the 1995 NBA Finals had an average height of six feet nine inches (205cm).

"We're guys that have to be on top of everything," says Phoenix Suns guard Elliot Perry. "Basketball players are the best-conditioned athletes because we have to run, we have to be strong. We have to weight-lift now. We have to be able to move in different directions at different speeds. I think that's what makes us feel we can always work on something and still apply it to basketball."

The brand of basketball played in the NBA is the fastest anywhere, but there is much more involved than a series of high-flying, fast-break dunks. Because such great players as Kareem Abdul-Jabbar, Oscar Robertson, and Larry Bird have appeared to score almost at will, there developed a common perception that defense was not a priority. "That's a myth," says Seattle SuperSonics coach George Karl. "The best defense played is in the NBA."

The 24-second shot clock mandates that teams operate with maximum efficiency on each possession, making quick, clear decisions despite the challenge presented by five capable defenders. Often, the approach used is to give the best scorers, players like Michael Jordan and Scottie Pippen of the Chicago Bulls, room to maneuver by shifting the other players to the opposite side of the court.

ABOVE: It was hustle and determination more than size or raw talent that made the Boston Celtics' Dave Cowens a Hall of Fame center and two-time NBA champion. OPPOSITE: At home in the O-rena, Shaquille O'Neal and the Orlando Magic routinely turn away challenges presented by players and teams like Shawn Respert and the Milwaukee Bucks. Orlando won more than 85 percent of its home games during the 1995–1996 season.

When scoring began to drop in the 1993–1994 season, however, with the New York Knicks and Houston Rockets averaging just 86 points apiece in the NBA Finals, the league passed rules limiting the ability of defensive players to use their hands on defense, and also moved the line for the three-point goal from nearly twenty-four feet (7.3m) at some points to just over twenty-one feet (6.4m) all the way around. Teams moved toward systems in which the ball is passed inside to the center—drawing guards or forwards in to double-team the big man and stop him from scoring—and then back out beyond the three-point line to the open player. The change made Orlando forward Dennis Scott an important weapon for his team, and reinforced the star status of Indiana Pacers guard Reggie Miller.

After a short period during which dominant centers were not considered important to winning teams, the three-point line caused teams to spread their offenses,

ABOVE: Madison Square Garden was originally solely used for college basketball games. Now both St. John's Red Storm and the New York Knicks call the Garden home. OPPOSITE: Player-coach Bill Russell blocks a shot by Laker Keith Erickson in the final game of the 1969 NBA finals. The Celtics won the game, 108–106, making them world champions for the eleventh time in the previous thirteen years.

and made big men who could maneuver with the ball, pass, and score—like Hakeem Olajuwon of the Houston Rockets and Shaquille O'Neal of the Orlando Magic— even more valuable.

The NBA has changed plenty in the last two decades. Before 1979, the NBA was considered to be out of touch with the average sports fan, too drug-infested to be of interest. The championship series was not carried live on television; it was tape-delayed, following the evening news in most places. Then along came Larry Bird to the Boston Celtics, Earvin "Magic" Johnson to the Los Angeles Lakers, and David Stern to the NBA commissioner's office.

With a strict anti-drug policy, a progressive labor agreement, and all the star power a league could want, the NBA grew furiously through the 1980s on the strength of the Celtics-Lakers rivalry. They met three times in the NBA Finals, and between them won eight championships from 1980 to 1988. As that rivalry cooled off, the game continued growing into the 1990s. When the Orlando Magic, Minnesota Timberwolves, Charlotte Hornets, and Miami Heat were added to the league in 1988, their franchises were purchased for less than $35 million each. When the league voted to expand again in 1994, this time breaking into Canada with the Vancouver Grizzlies and the Toronto

Cincinnati Royals guard Oscar Robertson was the only player ever to average a triple-double for an entire season.

Raptors, the two new teams each paid $125 million. After completing those deals, Stern talked about the possibility of placing the next new team in Mexico City, making the NBA the first U.S. sport to have a franchise south of the border.

Pro basketball has made astounding progress from its beginnings as a gimmick to fill arena dates and make their owners money. In 1946, the owner of the Boston Garden and others from Toronto and Detroit decided that pro hockey wasn't keeping them busy enough and, taking an idea from newspaper sports editor Max Kase, decided to attempt the formation of a pro basketball league. Ned Irish, of New York's Madison Square Garden, wasn't all that interested because of his success promoting college basketball, but he didn't want anyone else running the game in "his" building, and he agreed to join the new venture.

Knicks played at the Garden attracted a crowd of 17,205. In 1948, commissioner Maurice Podoloff convinced the Minneapolis Lakers (with their top drawing card George Mikan) and the Ft. Wayne Pistons of the rival National Basketball League to jump leagues. Thus the National Basketball Association was officially born.

The league progressed from walking to running in 1954, after too many teams had spent too much time standing around in too many games. There was one game in 1950 that ended with Ft. Wayne beating Minneapolis 19–18. Not all games were quite that dull, but there was enough inaction that the NBA owners decided to take some initiative. Syracuse Nationals owner Danny Biasone examined statistics from the 1953–1954 season and determined that teams averaged a shot every 18 seconds. He reasoned that a 24-second shot clock would therefore provide an appropriate amount of time to attack the basket on offense while eliminating stalling from the game. In the first season, scoring increased by 17 percent. The NBA became a fast-break league.

Pro basketball has been ruled through much of its history by the Boston Celtics, who won their first championship in 1956–1957 and have since won fifteen more, the first eleven with center Bill Russell as the key. Two more followed in the 1970s with Hall of Famers Dave Cowens and John Havlicek starring, and three in the 1980s were led by the front line of Larry Bird, Robert Parrish, and Kevin McHale.

It became almost impossible to repeat as champions after the Celtics won two in a row in 1968 and 1969, but in recent years it has become almost impossible not to: the Los Angeles Lakers won in 1987 and 1988, the Detroit Pistons in 1989 and 1990, the Chicago Bulls in 1991, 1992, and 1993, and then the Houston Rockets in 1994 and 1995. The excuse for failing to repeat in years past had been that the reigning champions were burdened by satisfaction and by having to serve as the target for the league's other teams. Now, champions carry an aura of greatness that is hard to deflate. The Celtics no longer stand as the NBA's only dynasty.

"I meet older guys now who got to watch Muhammad Ali fight, who have seen Gale Sayers run for a touchdown, who saw Bill Russell win championships in a row, in a row, in a row. I'm amazed by that," says Los Angeles Lakers forward Cedric Ceballos. "I am punished because I was too young to see all that.

"Now, I'm getting phone calls from Michael or Shaq to talk about basketball, and it's unbelievable. I'm a kid at this and I hope I stay a kid. This could all end for me tomorrow. They could realize I'm a fluke and I should never have been in the league, and they could kick me out. And if they do, I had a great time while I was here, got as many autographs as I could, and shook as many hands. I can tell my kids I played with the best of the best."

This group, along with representatives from such cities as Pittsburgh and Providence, formed the Basketball Association of America. At the first meeting, the decision was made to have games consist of four 12-minute quarters so they would run for two hours with breaks between quarters and halftime—now, with television commercials, it's closer to two and a half hours—and also decreed there would be no zone defenses. The first game the New York

The Ultimate Hoops Junkie

He is sweating. If there is a basketball game in the vicinity, you can be certain he is sweating. It is hard work being as happy as Dick Vitale. "For a guy who loves the game like me, it's just great to sit in that seat and watch all these great games."

Vitale is a television basketball analyst for ESPN and ABC. He is paid a great deal of money to sit at courtside or in a studio and shout his love for the game into a microphone. ESPN carries more than 200 basketball games a year, and though he is not around for all of them, it's still a lot of yelling.

"College basketball is certainly the vehicle that opened doors for me," Vitale says. "I think what's been a key is that my enthusiasm comes across and identifies with the sport; it's like a perfect fit for me. I don't think calling tennis or golf would work for Dick Vitale."

"As ESPN has grown, my notoriety has gone with it," Vitale says. "It's just been incredible. For a basketball fanatic, ESPN has become a way of life."

Vitale helps those ESPN games he graces to stand out from the abundance of basketball on television. CBS, ABC, and, to a lesser extent, NBC all broadcast regular-season college games. In most cities, there are also local games, games in regional syndication, and still more on other cable sports channels. There are National Basketball Association games on Ted Turner's TNT and TBS cable stations during the week and on NBC during the weekend.

The wealth of televised basketball has created a subculture of hoops junkies. They will watch UC Santa Barbara play Long Beach State at midnight if ESPN is willing to show it. They will watch Wisconsin-Green Bay against Xavier at noon on Saturday. To these people, there is no such thing as too obscure. The Minnesota Timberwolves and Miami Heat on TNT? There is no such thing as too much.

Actor and basketball fanatic Jack Nicholson says he watches more than 100 games on TV per year, in addition to those he attends as a front-row season ticket holder for the Los Angeles Lakers. "I like to watch games on television, on tape late at night because I don't like commercials and all that stuff," Nicholson says. He is also a fan of the UCLA Bruins, following them to the NCAA Final Four in 1974 at Greensboro, North Carolina, and in 1995 at the Seattle Kingdome.

President Bill Clinton has become a hoopaholic, in part because his home-state team, the Arkansas Razorbacks, grew into a basketball power at about the same time he became America's most powerful politician. The Razorbacks made the Final Four three times in the 1990s, and Clinton was in the audience when they won the NCAA championship at the Charlotte Coliseum in 1994. As the players went through the ceremonial cutting of the nets, Clinton came from his private box to shake their hands on the court.

As hard as it is for him to believe, Vitale has become almost as well-known as Nicholson and Clinton. Broadcasting college basketball has made Vitale a millionaire, the author of five books, and in constant demand for speeches and appearances. A successful coach at the University of Detroit, Vitale was not so successful as coach of

Although he never had a great jump shot, Dick Vitale has become the ultimate college basketball broadcaster.

the Detroit Pistons. He was fired after 10 games in 1979, and went into television as a means of filling time while he waited to get back into coaching.

"I fell in love with it," Vitale says of his broadcasting experiment. He became well known for being loud, and for his catch phrases. "Awesome, baby!" will follow a spectacular play. "Get a T-O" is shouted when a team is in obvious need of a timeout. At the start of his career, Vitale's high volume offended some critics and viewers, who ripped Vitale as well as ESPN for keeping him around. "Of all the critics I've read, they never said I didn't know the game and I didn't do my homework. They said, 'He's loud, he talks a lot.' You don't have to go to Harvard to figure that out." Through the years, Vitale's infectious enthusiasm has worn down most of his detractors. The game has made him more popular, and he has returned the favor.

"People at the top always told me 'You're so enthusiastic, your love of the game comes out,'" Vitale says. "I think what's happened after X number of years, people out there said, 'You know what? The guy just loves the game.'"

When Duke and Arkansas played for the 1994 NCAA championship, it was the most widely viewed college basketball game in history.

Made-for-TV

Only those who can fit twelve thousand of their closest friends into their living rooms can hope to watch a basketball game on television and duplicate the experience of being in a crowded, excited arena. Basketball nevertheless has proven to be the ideal TV sport.

The game sacrifices only a smidgen of its charm when squeezed onto a twenty-five-inch (64cm) diagonal screen, and none of the action is hidden. Whereas baseball and football broadcasts cannot incorporate all of the players who are on the field, televised basketball keeps all ten players in view most of the time. The games fit into comfortable time slots of two or two and a half hours. And the amount of last-second excitement surpasses the great finishes available in any other sport. Television has worked equally well in spreading the gospel of the college and professional game.

Those who have taken it upon themselves to analyze and interpret the dramatic rise in basketball's popularity generally have been content to assign most of the credit to Larry Bird and Magic Johnson for creating the explosion and to Michael Jordan for sustaining it.

It is true that the 1979 NCAA Championship game, in which Johnson's Michigan State Spartans defeated Bird's Indiana State Sycamores, stands as the highest-rated college basketball game ever, but it is not the most-watched. The audience for the 1979 title game, with 17.9 million homes, was far smaller than the 21.3 million that saw Arkansas beat Duke on CBS-TV in the 1994 championship. Starting with UCLA's victory against Memphis in 1973, NBC was drawing excellent ratings for the title game. Average attendance at tournament games rose from 11,914 in 1979 to 19,257 in 1987. So college basketball was already gaining popularity when Bird and Johnson came along, and it continued to grow long after they were gone.

Perhaps the single most dynamic agent in the growth of college basketball was the ESPN cable network, which used the game as inexpensive and entertaining programming to build its credibility and audience base as the first twenty-four-hour sports station. Before ESPN came along in 1979, nationally televised weekday college games were non-existent. There were only a couple of games each weekend on NBC, which then paid less than $5 million a year for the rights to the NCAA Tournament. Now, ESPN broadcasts more than 200 college games each winter, only part of the feast available to the sport's fans.

"When I first started, did the first game ever, DePaul and Wisconsin, you said you were working for ESPN and people would say, 'What is that?'" says network analyst Dick Vitale. "Now, everywhere we go, we're treated like royalty. ESPN has played a big, big role in the growth of the sport. In addition to seeing the really visible programs, the North Carolinas and the UCLAs, now all of a sudden everybody was on TV. I think ESPN allowed that to happen."

Television nonetheless affected the balance of power in both the professional and college game. After forming in time for the 1979–1980 season, the Big East Conference was the first college league to recognize the potential of television in general and of ESPN in particular. So many of the league's games were on TV that players from California who had no idea what Syracuse, New York, looked like wanted to play for the Orangemen. The Big East, for a short period, became the most powerful college basketball league, placing a record three teams in the 1985 Final Four: St. John's, Georgetown, and champion Villanova. Only when ESPN's schedule expanded and more leagues had their games shown were the Big Ten and Atlantic Coast Conference able to move back towards the top.

The situation was similar in the pros. In the early 1980s, when Bird was leading the Boston Celtics, Johnson was a force for the Los Angeles Lakers, and Julius Erving was still a star with the Philadelphia 76ers, CBS-TV began to focus its cameras on the teams that brought the highest ratings and had the broadest national appeal. This angered other teams in the league, and left great players like Dominique Wilkins of the Atlanta Hawks and Alex English of Denver in relative obscurity, but it helped draw more fans. It also made the Boston and Los Angeles players happy to stay in place and keep their teams in power.

In addition, the NBA decided to change its season calendar, moving back the start of the season so the championship series would fall in the month of June, away from the May ratings period the networks valued. This encouraged CBS to move the championship games out of the late-night, tape-delay ghetto to which they'd been consigned in 1980 and 1981. The value of the NBA telecasts had more than quadrupled by the time NBC won the rights to broadcast the games into the 1990s, and the NBA got still more from its cable contract with Ted Turner's TNT network.

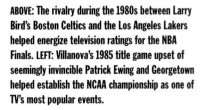

ABOVE: The rivalry during the 1980s between Larry Bird's Boston Celtics and the Los Angeles Lakers helped energize television ratings for the NBA Finals. LEFT: Villanova's 1985 title game upset of seemingly invincible Patrick Ewing and Georgetown helped establish the NCAA championship as one of TV's most popular events.

CBS, meanwhile, was spending a bigger bundle on the NCAA Tournament. The network had split the tournament with ESPN through the 1980s, but after seeing how viewers responded to the early-round games on cable, CBS bought the entire event, from the first round through the Final Four, for $1 billion. On weekday afternoons in mid-March, CBS began replacing *The Young and the Restless* with first-round NCAA games between the likes of Tulane and St. John's. When that seven-year contract still had three years to run, CBS renegotiated and paid $1.7 billion to hold the NCAA Tournament until the year 2002. It was the highest rights fee ever paid for a sporting event.

"We wanted to plan on having it, invest in it, make it part of the fabric of what is CBS Sports," said CBS Sports president David Kenin. "We're aggressively planning our future. We wanted this as part of it."

CHAPTER TWO

The Offensive End

The object of the game is to put the ball in the basket. College and pro coaches still say this all the time, as obvious as it may be to anyone who pays attention to the game. Usually, they say this on evenings when putting the ball in the basket has been more of a chore than usual.

The simplest element of basketball is the shot. "You can always just pick up a ball," says Houston Rockets forward Robert Horry, "and go shoot by yourself." And still it is as difficult to master as any part of the game. Players can work for years to develop a consistent jump shot, find that touch for a while, then lose it almost in an instant. Some players who play professionally for years, such as Charles Jones, Horry's teammate on the 1995 NBA champions, never really grow comfortable shooting the basketball.

A player with this flaw will make his contributions to the offense in other ways: by rebounding to get the ball for the players who can score, by setting screens to get them open, perhaps with passes that put them in position to score.

There is far more to the offensive end of the court than standing still and shooting the ball at the goal. At the game's highest level, players must invent or improvise unexpected means of getting into scoring range.

To reach the highest level, they must learn to pass, dribble, maybe to dunk, and certainly to convert fast-break layups. Most of the best players can score on some variety of a hook shot, although few can duplicate the precision instrument that was Kareem Abdul-Jabbar's sky hook. The introduction of the 3-point shot to professional and college basketball has made outside shooting more lucrative, but that hasn't made players better at it. There are just as few as ever who can reliably shoot from long distances.

Coaches diagram all manner of plays to set up their players for jumpers or layups, but those plans can be rendered unnecessary by a flash of offensive brilliance from one particular player or spoiled by a tight defensive effort from the opposing team.

The best individual scorers learn they aren't worth a lot if they can't help to make their team better. Only five times in history has the NBA's leading scorer led his team to the championship: Joe Fulks with Philadelphia in 1946, Abdul-Jabbar with Milwaukee in 1971, and Michael Jordan with the Chicago Bulls from 1991 to 1993. In college basketball, it's only happened once: Clyde Lovellette with Kansas in 1952.

"The bottom line," says University of Massachusetts coach John Calipari, "is that you have to mesh your skills with the four other players."

FAR LEFT: Orlando point guard Penny Hardaway has the necessary moves to get by Dallas guard Jason Kidd for a layup, but places more value on the passing skills that make him essential to his team.
LEFT: It sometimes takes three players—Horace Grant, Shaquille O'Neal, and Nick Anderson of Orlando—to stop a scorer as proficent as Houston's Hakeem Olajuwon.

Ballhandling

Long before Sean Miller became respected as a basketball player, he was famous for what he could do with a basketball. Miller was not yet a teenager when his talent for dribbling the ball earned him a guest appearance on NBC's Tonight Show. Miller stopped bouncing balls only long enough to shake hands with Johnny Carson himself.

By his tenth birthday, Miller could do anything imaginable with a basketball, from dribbling several at once to dribbling at high speeds through his legs and around his back to spinning a number of balls on his fingers. The son of a successful western Pennsylvania high school coach, Miller learned these skills not so that he could perform circus acts, but to one day be a great player. Miller eventually became a four-year starter at point guard for the University of Pittsburgh.

He is the career leader in assists at Pitt. There is no statistic than can measure ballhandling ability, but Miller probably would not have been a top college player without

it. He grew to be only six feet (183cm) tall, but dribbling is the one skill in basketball that may be enhanced by being closer to the ground.

"I was able to be around the gym a lot and always have the basketball in my hands when I was a kid," Miller says. "Because you're little and can't reach the basket, you tend to keep the ball dribbling more than anything.

"What being able to handle the ball well does is enable you to really see the court. A lot of times, when you wonder why guys in general can't pass or see the floor, a lot of times it becomes that they've got to get their steering wheel intact first; if they're worried about dribbling with their left hand, they're not going to see the guy down the court. I never had to worry about the ball. My thoughts were on other things: my teammates, the defender in front of me, how fast everything's moving."

From the time when Marques Haynes of the Harlem Globetrotters was putting on amazing displays of his ballhandling skills in the 1950s, great dribbling has been seen by some as a pointless act of showmanship, and by other

ABOVE: Players as such as Scottie Pippen and B.J. Armstrong are often too tall to have an answer for the dribbling skills presented by five-foot-three-inch (160cm) point guard Muggsy Bogues of the Charlotte Hornets. OPPOSITE: Former Detroit Pistons guard Isiah Thomas moved as fast while dribbling the ball as most opponents did when sprinting.

Los Angeles Lakers star Magic Johnson, using his six-foot-nine-inch (206cm) body to back down Michael Jordan, may be the tallest great ballhandler in history.

basketball purists as a self-indulgent waste of time. When college basketball rules changed in the 1990s to allow players to dribble more, Kansas coach Roy Williams complained bitterly, because he favored forcing players to keep the ball moving among their teammates with passes.

Pete Newell, the legendary coach of the 1959 NCAA champion California team, claims overuse of the dribble renders the other four players on offense useless. Isiah Thomas, the star point guard who led the Detroit Pistons to the NBA championship in 1989 and 1990, says players should never dribble the ball without a purpose.

Being able to move quickly while dribbling the ball, though, is what makes Tyrone "Muggsy" Bogues capable of playing in the NBA despite being only five feet three inches (160cm) tall. The gift for changing directions quickly while dribbling and executing shocking passes on the move helped make a Hall of Fame player out of "Pistol" Pete Maravich, who played with the Atlanta Hawks and the New Orleans Jazz in the NBA and scored more points in three college seasons than any other player did in four. His ability to dribble the ball with great skill despite standing six feet eight inches (203cm) made Magic Johnson the greatest point guard of all time.

Players have become better ballhandlers in the 1990s, able to do more things at higher speeds, largely because officials gradually changed their interpretation of rules against carrying the ball on the dribble. It used to be that dribblers were required to keep their hands on top of the ball, but flashy, quick guards like Tim Hardaway of the Golden State Warriors and Kevin Johnson of the Phoenix Suns have learned to change directions on the run by placing their hands on the sides of the basketball and bouncing it from there. Only when players lose control of the dribble are they called for palming.

"You have different types of ballhandlers," says Milwaukee Bucks guard Shawn Respert. "I'm not a fancy ballhandler. I'm a control ballhandler, a smart ballhandler. When the right pass needs to be made, that's the stuff I try to do."

Respert had to work diligently to become a competent ballhandler. He entered college at Michigan State known for his ability to shoot and score, but at six feet two inches (187cm), he realized he would have to have the skills of a point guard to make it in the NBA.

"A lot of times, I'd be able to drive by guys, but then I'd get the ball knocked out of my hand, or be out of control and make a bad pass. When I started to learn to get the ball out front and go past people while I kept the ball out front, there weren't too many people who could stay with me. That's when my game started to develop, because the guys had to respect me for the drive and the outside shot."

Maravich, born in the small steel town of Aliquippa, not far from Miller's home, is the player who made popular the value of ballhandling drills. He worked constantly from the time he was little, and got so good with the ball that he could make bounce passes turn left or right at ninety-degree angles. The gimmick Miller used to develop as a dribbler was to constantly bounce two balls at once, forcing himself to grow accustomed to using his left hand with-

out concentrating on it. Ask Orlando Magic all-star guard Anfernee Hardaway what made him such a gifted ballhandler, and he has no answer. He is six feet seven inches (200cm) tall, the tallest great point guard since Johnson, but he believes his basketball skills were natural.

"It was just totally God-gifted," Hardaway says. "I didn't think I'd ever grow to be as tall as six foot seven, but once I did, my skills just stayed with me. I never worked on ballhandling in my life. I can handle the ball against a smaller guy and get it up the court, and a bigger guy that's trying to guard me, I can get around him with the ballhandling. I never have to think about it. I just come down the court and do something, and I go on about my business."

As the jump to professional basketball approached, Milwaukee guard Shawn Respert worked tirelessly to improve his dribbling skills, so he would be comfortable as a point guard.

Guard Tim Hardaway's patented crossover dribble move is considered one of the most dazzling, dizzying offensive weapons in the NBA.

Passing

He has scored thousands of points, more per game than any player who has competed in the National Basketball Association. He has won three NBA championships and two Olympic gold medals, made a fortune endorsing sneakers, underwear, and hamburgers. What else could Michael Jordan want? "I wish I could pass like Magic."

For all the excitement that dunking brings to basketball, there is nothing as breathtaking as a perfectly thrown pass. If it is done behind the back or over the shoulder or between three defenders, all the better. Magic Johnson did this and more during his career with the Los Angeles Lakers. If he is not the greatest passer in the sport's history, he is certainly the greatest player to make passing his specialty. Johnson held the NBA career assists record until it was broken by John Stockton of the Utah Jazz in 1995. His passing probably extended the career of the great Kareem Abdul-Jabbar, and it definitely helped forward James Worthy through a career that one day will land him in the Hall of Fame.

Although he eventually decided that passing was his favorite part of the game, and is proud to have young players seek to emulate this skill, Johnson admits, "I wasn't always so unselfish." He was easily the best player on his youth teams, and so would think nothing of scoring 26 points in a game if his team got a total of 30. The parents of the other players were not pleased, and sometimes their sons weren't either. "As I got older, maybe twelve, I realized I could be happy and make the other guys happy, too," Johnson once said. "I decided to let the other kids score. I figured they'd be happy they scored, and we'd win, which would make me happy. Winning is what it's all about."

Basketball is the ultimate team game because cooperation among the five players isn't mandated, only preferred. An offensive tackle on a football team can't alter the game so that his role is more prominent. A power forward can, but with successful teams, he generally does what is required and what comes his way. Selflessness makes for championship teams, and is best reflected in the pass.

As if to demonstrate the value of sharing the ball, the NBA has been keeping track of assists as long as it has kept scoring statistics, from Ernie Calverly of the Providence Steamrollers in 1946–1947 to Stockton, today's reigning king of playmaking. Stockton became the first player to top 10,000 career assists, but, befitting a player whose specialty is giving up the glory, he called the record "just a stat." In overtaking Johnson and the legendary Oscar Robertson to claim the mark, Stockton seemed almost embarrassed to be in their company. This was a guy who came out of tiny Gonzaga University in Washington State figuring he wouldn't make the NBA. "Those guys are historical players who did so many things, and I don't fit into that category, quite honestly."

The best of passers sometimes have trouble explaining what they do, and the best of passes happen so quickly that no one else can either. Someone like Kenny Anderson of the New Jersey Nets, standing beyond the free throw line, will spot an opening about to develop inside and snap off a pass to teammate Derrick Coleman before anyone on the other team can react.

The best of all passers also have an incredible feel for where the other players on the court are positioned, even in moments of mass confusion. When he was still at the University of Memphis, NBA all-star guard Anfernee Hardaway of the Orlando Magic demonstrated this instinct in a

ABOVE: Los Angeles guard Magic Johnson set the NBA career assists record while leading the Lakers to five world championships. RIGHT: As a first-year Memphis State player, Penny Hardaway was already being compared to Magic Johnson.

game against Marquette University. After one of Hardaway's teammates missed a free throw, the ball was knocked loose on the floor, and players from both sides scrambled after it. Hardaway chased it down and wound up sitting on the floor with the ball in his lap, his legs facing the opposite end of the court. In a flash, Hardaway directed the ball with his right hand over his left shoulder, directly to teammate Billy Smith beneath the Memphis basket; Smith was fouled as he attempted to shoot. Hardaway calls it his favorite play in two seasons of playing for the Tigers.

Detroit Pistons forward Grant Hill is shown here passing for his college team, Duke. However, while at Duke, Hill was usually on the receiving end of passes from Bobby Hurley, the career assist leader in NCAA Division I ball.

One reason is because he didn't get yelled at for choosing to pass. Hardaway loves to distribute the ball among his teammates so much that he risked the wrath of his coaches in junior high, high school, and college, each of whom wanted Hardaway to take more shots. He hears that less now, since one of his teammates with the Magic is seven-foot-one-inch (215cm) all-star center Shaquille O'Neal.

A player doesn't have to be a Johnson or Stockton or Hardaway to gain value as a passer. Corey Beck was the point guard for the 1994 Arkansas team that won the NCAA championship. He doesn't have the creative skills those others are blessed with, but he helped make teammate Corliss Williamson an All-American, teammate Scotty Thurman all–Southeastern Conference, and all his teammates winners. "It's really a matter of being smart on the court, being able to find the open man at the right time," Beck said. "I know how to find that guy and get him the ball when he's got the chance to score."

In a thirteen-year career split between the ABA and NBA, Ron Boone averaged 3.7 assists—plenty for a shooting guard who scored nearly 17,500 points. He never thought of himself as much of a passer while in col-

lege at Idaho State, and didn't work hard to make himself one. He just blended with his teammates on the Utah Stars; Boone played on an ABA championship team in 1971. "We were a running team and got out and pushed the ball up the court; you just developed. You turned into a guy that would hit the open man. It just came naturally because of our style of play."

There have been teams that won the NBA championship without great center play or overwhelming rebounding or a terrific shot-blocker in the middle. The Chicago Bulls won three in a row in the 1990s while lacking all three. No team has won the title without being able to share the basketball. The 1977 Portland Trail Blazers were among the best-passing teams in pro basketball history, in part because they had the best-passing big man in center Bill Walton. His ability to move the ball through the offense did not provide him with a great number of assists, but "he no doubt made it work," says former Trail Blazers teammate Larry Steele.

"He was a tremendous passer and a tough player. You've got to be quick on the trigger, and he could do that. You've got to be able to see, evaluate, and make the play really fast. You can't teach people to do that. They're just born with that tendency to develop the game in that direction. You've got to be quick and react spontaneously."

The Free Throw

It is a moment of respite in a game of perpetual motion, a simple, colorless act in a sport that increasingly has come to value flamboyance.

The free throw is out of style.

Which is not the same as being worthless.

It is possible that nothing in basketball is as agonizingly dramatic as a free throw fired with a game on the line and no time on the clock. The most enduring recent memory of this occurred in the 1989 NCAA championship game, when Michigan guard Rumeal Robinson was fouled on a drive and made 2 free throws to defeat Seton Hall in overtime, 80–79. Otherwise, free throws are dull. People who watch televised basketball games on videotape have learned to fast-forward through the free throws and determine whether or not they were made by checking the score as the ball is advanced upcourt. Just as spectators don't care to watch free throws being shot, players don't care to practice them.

"If you watch guys play in the off-season, very seldom will you see anybody shooting free throws," says former coach Hugh Durham, who took Florida State to the Final Four in 1972 and Georgia in 1983. "You see them dunking and dribbling behind the back and shooting fadeaway jumpers and three-pointers from NBA range."

Although coaches complain that players don't shoot free throws well and don't practice them diligently enough,

THE AGE OF THE GUNNER

Austin Carr, one of basketball's great gunners, puts up a shot over Duquesne's Mike Barr.

No one complained. 'At least not publicly. Nobody said too much about it." Austin Carr kept shooting, and his teammates at Notre Dame either passed him the ball or watched. He'd fire nearly 30 times a game, but no one bothered him because he made the majority of his shots and because what he was doing was the order of the day in college basketball. He was a gunner.

For a brief period in the college game's hundred-year history, from 1967 through 1973, it became fashionable for talented guards to shoot whenever they were open. The more they made, the more they shot. On the playground, players who refuse to pass the ball and keep firing at the basket are called "gunners" or "chuckers." Pistol Pete Maravich made that designation a genuine compliment.

Maravich played at Louisiana State University from 1967 through 1970. A six-foot-five-inch (195cm) guard, he was one of the most gifted passers and ballhandlers ever to play the game, but because he played for his father, Press Maravich, and because his teammates weren't as talented, he was encouraged to shoot as often as necessary. That worked out to 40 times per game. In 1969–1970, his senior season, Maravich shot 1,168 times—just 359 fewer than the entire Ohio State team, which led the nation in shooting percentage.

"It was in vogue to be a high scorer at the time," Carr says. "The coaches didn't mind having one or two players score the majority of the points. I didn't look at it as shooting a lot, because I always shot over 55 percent from the field. It's just the way our offense was set up."

In another time, another era of basketball, Carr would no doubt have been a great player, an All-American. Instead, he became a legend, because he played at that point in history when it was not deemed unreasonable or even selfish for one player to take most of the shots. More than two decades later, this is Carr's best defense for his great offensive skills: "If a player was open, I would get him the ball. I wouldn't pass up an open player to get a shot."

He didn't have to worry about that much, though. He was open often enough to shoot nearly 30 times per game his senior season, and proficient enough as a marksman to make 52 percent of his shots. Carr averaged 38 points per game in 1970–1971—and he didn't even lead college basketball in scoring. Johnny Neumann was a sophomore at Mississippi that season and averaged 40.1 points on 34 shots per game.

The year before, Carr averaged 38.1 points but lost the college scoring title to Maravich, who scored 44.5 points per game as a senior, but Carr did set the NCAA Tournament single-season scoring record with 61 points in a 112–82 win against Ohio University. He later had to do some explaining when his son learned Carr had taken 44 shots in setting that record.

"I got going basically out of necessity," Carr says. "The guy I played against, John Canine, hit his first 6 shots that game, and my coach asked me if I was going to play any defense. Everything was a blur after that. It was just my day. I took 44 shots that game, but I made 25 of them. That was just the way it was."

In 1969–1970, when Maravich and Carr were at the top of the scoring list, Purdue's Rick Mount was good for 35.4 points a game. At Niagara, Calvin Murphy shot better but less often than he did as a junior, and slipped from 32.4 points to 29.4.

When Carr, Mount, and Maravich were gone, long-bombing Dwight Lamar of Southwestern Louisiana led the colleges in scoring at 36.3 in 1972. As he was succeeded by William "Bird" Averitt at Pepperdine (33.9) in 1973, though, it became clear the trend was beginning to die out. It wasn't so much because there weren't any great-shooting guards who could be trusted to cut loose so often, it just didn't seem like the thing to do any longer.

"I guess it was basically because they couldn't find players who could sustain that," says Carr. "You've got to be in great condition, and you've got

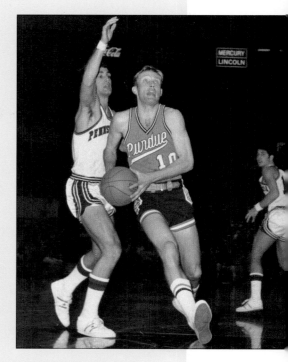

Rick Mount shot his way from high school legend in Lebanon, Indiana, to college phenomenon at Purdue.

to be able to make a lot of shots. The outside jump shooter, a guy who could dominate like that, started to wane, and the play started to focus inside more. I just think the style of the game changed."

ABOVE, LEFT: The most celebrated free throw in recent seasons was shot by Michigan guard Rumeal Robinson to win the 1989 NCAA Championship over Seton Hall. ABOVE: When Rick Barry tries to convince young players his underhand free throw style is the most efficent means of shooting, they resist because it looks funny.

rarely do those coaches employ players based on their ability to hit from the foul line. Coaches continue to stress rebounding, shooting, passing, and defense, which is one reason players pay the most attention to those aspects of the game. Most college and pro coaches spend little of their precious practice time correcting bad free throw habits. "I try to get our guys to take it personally, and to work on their own," says Nolan Richardson, coach of the Arkansas Razorbacks team that won the 1994 NCAA championship.

"It's not one of the glamorous parts of the game any more," says Austin Carr, who scored 10,473 points—1,753 of them on free throws—during a ten-year career with the Cleveland Cavaliers. "In high school, my coach said, 'Son, this is a shot that nobody is going to stop you from shooting, and you should focus on it.' The only difference in the free throw motion and the jumpshot is the routine."

Great free throw shooters generally have routines they follow before shooting that can never be interrupted. The routine is as much a part of the shot as the release of the ball. Adrian Dantley, a 20,000-point scorer in fifteen seasons with Utah and Detroit, among others, used to wrap his hand and forearm over the ball and spin it backward toward his chin, then bring the ball to his forehead and shoot. Kyle Macy, who played with the Phoenix Suns in the early 1980s, always wiped his hands on his socks to make sure they were dry. Indiana Pacers guard Mark

Jackson raises his right arm in front of him and points his fingers at the rim, aiming at his target. Rick Barry, a forward who was inducted to the Hall of Fame, made 90 percent of his free throws by tossing them underhanded.

"I got to the point when I was shooting them, I used to shoot them on my knees, too, and make them," says Larry Finch, a star guard at the University of Memphis in the early 1970s. "That's just confidence. You've got to have that kind of confidence that comes through shooting the ball over and over and over, until the ball becomes an extension of your hand."

College players from the early 1960s through the late 1980s were reasonably accurate free throw shooters, generally making between 68 and 69 percent of their attempts, hitting a high of 69.7 percent in 1979. Free throw accuracy has declined dramatically during the 1990s. College players in 1991 made 68.5 percent of their foul shots; by 1995, it was 66.9 percent. In the NBA, players in 1975 made 76.4 percent from the foul line. By 1994, it was 73.4 percent.

Players such as Chris Dudley of the Portland Trail Blazers have become famous for their misadventures at the line. He shot 36 percent in his second season with the Cleveland Cavaliers, 32 percent in his third. In recent years, he has lifted his average above the .500 mark. Jerome Lane, a forward who played with Denver and Cleveland in the late 1980s and early 1990s, has two listings in the NBA record book for most free throw attempts, none made, in a game. He ranks third (8) and fourth (7).

Of course, horrible free throw shooting is nothing new. Wilt Chamberlain, the greatest scoring machine in basketball history, also set the standard by which lousy foul shooters would be measured. He made only 51.1 percent in his NBA career. Had he shot 75 percent, about average for his era, his lifetime scoring average would have risen from 30.1 points to 32.8, which would place him ahead of the leader in that category, Michael Jordan.

David Robinson of the San Antonio Spurs stresses keeping his shooting hand behind the ball and his eyes on the target when firing from the line.

Chamberlain tried just about every method imaginable to break his lifelong slump, though. He moved to the side of the line, to the back of the circle, shot them underhanded. Nothing worked. Among the vast number of records he holds is that for the most free throw attempts in a single game without making one: 10.

Jump Shots and Three-Pointers

"It used to be dunks," says Houston Rockets forward Robert Horry, who has earned two NBA championship rings. "Now, it's three-pointers. That's basically how things change."

This is the abbreviated history of basketball in Horry's young lifetime. He grew up as a lean, agile forward who could easily jump and dunk the ball, but by the time he got to the NBA, he was far more valuable for his ability to shoot from a long distance. Few expected Horry to be a great pro player when he left the University of Alabama, but still fewer knew he could shoot the three-pointer.

"I've been shooting like that ever since I was in high school," Horry says. "I always had the touch. My high school coach, he's the one that gave me the form to shoot the ball. Keep your elbows in, keep the ball above your head, don't let the ball sit in the palm of your shooting hand, just release it. Just let it go."

Ron Boone, a high-scoring guard with the Utah Stars of the American Basketball Association, believes sound form is the most important aspect of the jump shot. "If you see a guy with good form, nine out of ten times he can develop into a good shooter. How many guys in the NBA do you see now that do not have good form? Nowadays, 95 percent of the players have good form."

Shooting is the most elementary basketball skill, however, the one nearly everyone attempts before moving to more advanced aspects of the game or giving it up altogether. Although Horry accurately describes the fundamentals of a proper jump shot, the way a player shoots is a kind of personal statement about how (and sometimes when) he or she grew to feel comfortable playing. To keep his son, Jaron, from picking up bad habits, Ron Boone started him off shooting a volleyball, which was lighter and easier to grip than a basketball. Jaron developed a picture-perfect jump shot and became a top guard at the University of Nebraska whose specialty was long-range shooting.

The younger a player became proficient, the more likely it is that that person will only look like a great shooter as the ball goes through the basket. Guard Kenny Smith, who went from the playgrounds of New York to the University of North Carolina to a couple of world championships with the Houston Rockets, puts a sideways spin on the ball and involves his left thumb in the release instead of merely using his left hand as a guide. He can be a streaky shooter because of this, but he regularly makes about 40 percent of his three-point attempts, and has never failed to average double-figure scoring in nearly a decade of playing in the NBA.

Star guard Reggie Miller of the Indiana Pacers keeps his elbows wide and pushes the ball off his guiding hand with an odd, twisting flick of the wrist, and yet he is the most lethal long-range shooter in the NBA. When George Gervin was the leading scorer with the San Antonio Spurs in the 1970s and 1980s, his shot began with the ball wedged on his right ear. Unlike Miller, his release and follow-through were ideal. Gervin became the number twenty career scorer in NBA history with that shot, and scored 26,595 points with the Spurs and the Chicago Bulls.

To become a great shooter, then, it is more important for a player to be consistent with his motion than it is to have "correct" form. And the player must be confident. "The biggest thing, you've got to have a big heart and you've got to have that confidence," says forward Dennis Scott of the Orlando Magic, another of the game's great shooters.

"I think there are lots of times you just have to feel it," says Dallas Mavericks shooting guard Jimmy Jackson. "You have to catch it, step into it, and shoot it. Every time you catch the ball and think about it, it kind of takes away from the rhythm."

The ability to shoot without remorse is one reason Michael Jordan of the Chicago Bulls grew to become the player acknowledged as the greatest in the history of the game. His one-on-one scoring skills were so overwhelming that little he did was questioned. This enabled him to shoot often enough in games to gain great confidence in his ability.

"I think he did improve his outside shot," says Matt Doherty, Jordan's teammate on the 1982 NCAA championship team at North Carolina. "I don't want to say that was an area of weakness, because he was a very good shooter, but if he needed to work on one thing, that was it. I think the scouting report on Michael at first was to make him take a jump shot, don't let him drive by you because he was such a great athlete. I don't think that would work now."

ABOVE: Orlando guard Penny Hardaway pump-fakes to move Chicago Bulls defender Michael Jordan out of the play and clear his way for a jumpshot. OPPOSITE: No shot in basketball is tougher than the fadeaway jumper, but a shooting guard, like Jimmy Jackson of Dallas, has to have it in his repertoire.

No one looked more awkward shooting a basketball than George "The Iceman" Gervin, but he made more than 10,000 field goals in a fourteen-year Hall of Fame career.

Despite the shooting success of players like Gervin, Larry Bird of the Boston Celtics, and Alex English of the Denver Nuggets, and even Jordan and Drexler, there were many who believed the drive to dunk had taken the jump shot out of the game by the mid-1980s. The NBA had adopted the three-point shot in 1979, but now the colleges also decided to put the three-point rule in play. Starting in 1986–1987, college players were awarded three points for every shot longer than nineteen feet nine inches (6m). Indiana star guard Steve Alford used that rule to win an unexpected NCAA championship the first season it was in effect. The three-point rule has become an important aspect of the game for most successful teams.

The person most responsible for the three-point shot in college was the late Ed Steitz, who ran the NCAA rules committee from an office in the athletic department at Springfield College, the successor to the Springfield YMCA school where James A. Naismith had invented the game. Steitz said when the rule was passed that the idea was "to put the outside shooter back into the game." It has worked in that sense—more shots are taken from long range every season—but it has not led to the development of more great shooters. The three-point percentage for major college teams has declined each year.

Most successful players in the NBA are proficient shooters. Center Patrick Ewing of the New York Knicks entered the pros with a reputation as a player who could play great defense but could not score. He never averaged 18 points while playing in college at Georgetown. With the Knicks, though, he refined his jumper to produce a consistent touch from sixteen feet (4.8m) and in, and has never averaged fewer than 20 points per game. Star guard Clyde Drexler of the Houston Rockets was expected to be a dunking specialist when he entered the NBA. He made 1 three-point shot in his first season (1983–1984), but kept working until he hit 114 in his best season (1991–1992). Those who don't make shots don't make the grade.

"It definitely comes from practice, from working on your game, realizing your weakness and working on it," says Ron Boone, now a broadcast analyst with the Utah Jazz. "If you're not a good outside shooter, your opponents know it, and that's what they want to give you. So you spend your time in practice trying to work on proper form and building confidence. Eventually, as good an athlete as Patrick Ewing is, he turned into a good shooter."

Nearly a third of all shots in college basketball are three-pointers, but teams that allow themselves to be seduced by the apparent ease of hitting that jump shot often shoot themselves into an unexpected defeat. In 1995, UCLA won a championship while making only 2 three-point goals in each of its 2 games at the Final Four. "Some games you look back, and there are 20 three-point shots and 5 inside, and you say, 'Wait a minute. This isn't the way it's supposed to be,'" says UCLA coach Jim Harrick. "You shoot three-point shots, and I shoot layups, and I'm going to beat you almost every time."

The NBA three-point line was moved in from nearly twenty-four feet (7.3m) to just over twenty-one feet (6.4m) prior to the 1994–1995 season. Although it brought the shot within range of more players, it did not diminish the value of players who can shoot the three-pointer with confidence and precision. Players like Scott, Miller, and Horry are still rare, in part because their size enables them to get off the shot with more regularity. Miller and Horry are both six feet seven inches tall (200cm). Scott is six feet eight inches (203cm), but he has been a superior shooter since he played in high school.

Scott works incredibly hard to keep his touch. Before every game he plays for the Orlando Magic, he shoots for two hours. "People think I'm crazy, getting to the game three hours early to shoot, but it's something I've done all along." He fires 500 practice jumpers a day during the season.

"I think the biggest thing with me is, you always want to keep the follow-through," Scott says. "A lot of guys don't have the natural form of keeping the elbow in—like Reggie Miller. He doesn't have the great form, but at the end of every shot he always has that follow-through and has great concentration."

The Air Game

Connie Hawkins is one pioneer of flight who is rarely given his due. The Wright Brothers, Charles Lindbergh, Alan Shepherd—they get all the credit, all the glory, the airports and universities and streets named for them. Hawkins soared with the best, and he didn't even have a machine to help.

When the game of basketball was still bound to the ground, Hawkins came along in the early 1960s and lifted it to an altitude where it still operates today. He is a member of basketball's Hall of Fame, but Hawkins still is not as well known as some of those practitioners of his art who came later: Julius Erving, David Thompson, Dominique Wilkins, and Michael Jordan.

Hawkins had huge hands, long arms, and a creative feel for the game that no one before him had demonstrated. He could jump into the air with one play on his mind and change in mid-flight, slamming the ball through the goal and leaving his opponents bewildered. In the ABA's first season, he led the league in scoring, ranked second in rebounds, and fourth in assists. He didn't play in the NBA until he was twenty-seven because he was falsely implicated in a gambling scandal while a freshman at the University of Iowa. His banishment did not end until he settled a lawsuit against the NBA in 1969.

"Only the players really knew how good this guy was," says Roger Brown, Hawkins' friend from their playground days in Brooklyn, himself a great guard with the ABA's Indiana Pacers. "The game would have progressed a lot quicker with Connie as a star. People would have seen the air game, taking off from the foul line and dunking."

Dunking was not necessarily what everyone in the basketball establishment wanted. College rulesmakers outlawed the dunk in 1967, presumably as a reaction to the sophomore year dominance of UCLA Bruins center Lew Alcindor (now Kareem Abdul-Jabbar). There were those in the black community, however, who believed the decision had more to do with the ability of their smaller players to change the style of the game with their remarkable leaping ability.

TOP: Connie Hawkins was the ABA's first significant drawing card when he played for the Pittsburgh Pipers in 1967-1968. ABOVE: Clyde "The Glide" Drexler became known as a high-flying player at the University of Houston, then returned to the city to lead the Rockets to the 1995 NBA title.

Erving came along almost a decade later, and began to dazzle opponents and spectators in the New York area with his high-flying act. He never legally dunked a ball in a regulation college game, but he averaged 26.3 points and 20 rebounds at the University of Massachusetts. Still, he was relatively unknown when he signed with the ABA's Virginia Squires after his junior season in 1971.

As he played with the Squires, stories began to drift out of Virginia about his astounding dunks and improvisational style. His nickname, Dr. J, became widely known, but ABA games weren't on national television, and few could claim to have actually watched him play. After he won the league's slam-dunk contest at the 1976 All-Star Game in Denver, taking off from the foul line and throwing the ball through the basket on the winning dunk, fans in non-ABA cities were dying to see him. The ABA and NBA merged soon after, and there are still people who believe the NBA's desire to have Dr. J as a gate attraction forced the deal. The day it became clear Erving would be playing in the NBA, a Detroit autoworker walked into the Pistons' ticket office and handed his paycheck over to the clerk. "Give me all the tickets to Dr. J this will buy," he said.

In his sixteen-year pro career, Erving was an all-star sixteen times and played on champion teams in the ABA and NBA, but he is best remembered for convincing sports fans that basketball could be as exciting for its style as for its speed. In the 1980 NBA Finals against Los Angeles, Erving drove the baseline, jumped from the right side and floated along the length of the backboard to flick the ball off the left side of the board and into the goal. The tape of this play has been aired dozens of times, but it never becomes less astonishing. When asked long ago how he was able to conceive shots and dunks no one had seen before, he said, "It's easy, once you learn to fly."

David Thompson was an even greater leaper than Erving. Although he didn't have quite the same flair for the game and didn't last as long in the pros, his ability to jump above the opposition when he played for North Carolina State's 1974 NCAA champions led to the creation of the alley-oop, or lob play, that is common today. Rules never allowed Thompson to dunk in college, but he climbed so high he could look down into the basket and drop the ball in. Once, when playing in the 1974 NCAA Tournament against Pittsburgh, he had to leave the game with a head injury after falling headfirst to the floor. He had tripped on a teammate's shoulder.

At the University of Georgia and with the Atlanta Hawks, Dominique Wilkins became known as "The Human Highlight Film," using his gift of flight to average more than 25 points per game and make eight All-Star games.

Even someone who's done it as many times as Michael Jordan never tires of throwing down a vicious dunk to deflate his opponents.

Dominique Wilkins, considered one of the great aerial maneuverers, thrilled NBA fans such as these at Chicago with impressive dunks before taking his talents to Italy.

The ability to jump, to stay airborne, and to change a play in flight, however, is the thread that runs from Hawkins to Erving to Jordan. "Air Jordan" is considered history's greatest player because he can do at altitude what the other two can and also shoot better and play superior defense. Jordan helped North Carolina to an NCAA championship in 1982, as a freshman, and later brought the Chicago Bulls three consecutive NBA championships in the 1990s. "When he was still a freshman, Michael did some amazing things," says Matt Doherty, Jordan's North Carolina teammate. "He did things in practices and in games that would take your breath away. You knew he was going to be special."

In winning the first NBA title against the Los Angeles Lakers in 1991, Jordan is best remembered for a play on which he took off just inside the foul line intending to

THE HOOK SHOT

He was an idol to a generation of young basketball players, maybe even two, but it seems none of them wanted to be just like Kareem Abdul-Jabbar. His specialty was the hook shot, and it has just about disappeared from the game.

You will often see some using the hook-dunk or the jump-hook, which is launched with the player facing the basket and the ball curling off the fingers. Almost never does a player in the NBA or NCAA execute the rolling hook shot the way Abdul-Jabbar did so often through his two decades in the basketball spotlight.

Why? "Because it looks funny," says center Brad Daugherty of the Cleveland Cavaliers, who developed a decent hook and became an NBA all-star. "When you're growing up, nobody wants to shoot a hook shot. Everybody wants to shoot jump shots and pass behind the back. It just looks funny."

The hook the way Abdul-Jabbar used it, though, was a thing of simple beauty that slowly developed, like a flower grudgingly exposing its inner potential. He would catch a pass, swing his left foot forward and stretch toward the ceiling, his right arm extended and the ball clutched in his right hand. At the peak of this motion came a flick of the wrist. Abdul-Jabbar's specialty came to be known as the skyhook. It was the most devastating offensive move in the sport's history. Because the shooter's body is wedged perpendicularly between the ball and the defender, it is almost impossible to block.

"If I was guarding me, one-on-one? No, I couldn't stop it," says Abdul-Jabbar. "You can block it if you drop off someone else and come in from behind, but that's a different story."

The hook was developed in the 1920s, but became popular in the 1940s with such players as six-foot-nine-inch (205cm) Clyde Lovelette of the Minneapolis Lakers and six-foot-four-inch (193cm) Cliff Hagan of the St. Louis Hawks. It was Abdul-Jabbar, though, who perfected it. As he remembers it, no one taught him how to execute the hook properly. He used it when he was in fourth grade because it was the best way for him to get the ball to the basket. "I just started doing it," Jabbar says. "It's been part of my game since then."

Kurt Rambis, a six-foot-ten-inch (208cm) forward who was Abdul-Jabbar's teammate with the Los Angeles Lakers during the 1980s, says he gave up trying the hook because the zone defenses he faced during college at Santa Clara ganged up on him from behind when he tried to shoot it.

"When you're coming across with the hook shot, the ball's just sort of hanging out there, and too many players were stealing it," Rambis says. "You need a lot more room to get that shot off."

Fewer coaches teach the hook shot to younger players, even promising big men who could make great use of it. "Post men come into the NBA, and they're not shooting the hook," says Pat Riley, former coach of the Los Angeles Lakers and New York Knicks. "It's

turnaround jumpers, power moves, and stuff like that. I think Kareem is testimony that if a man works on that shot and develops it, it can be unstoppable. It does surprise me that more players don't utilize it."

One player who remains devoted to the hook shot is seven-foot (213cm) center George Zidek. Like Abdul-Jabbar, he played in college at UCLA, but, not surprisingly, he did not learn to play the game on America's playgrounds. He is from the former Czechoslovakia. Zidek used the hook as a weapon to help UCLA win the 1995 NCAA championship—he can make it with his right hand and his weaker left hand—and then became a first-round draft choice of the NBA's Charlotte Hornets.

Hagan says the difficulty in learning the shot is one reason players have abandoned it. "It's contrary to anything a player has done to that point. They don't have the patience to learn the feel. It's such a strange feeling. Players get pretty far along in basketball, and they think they're pretty good, and they don't like people throwing something at them they can't do."

Kareem Abdul-Jabbar, beating San Antonio center Artis Gilmore with a strong move to the goal, became so proficient with the skyhook he could launch it with either hand.

dunk with his right hand, but, finding that path blocked, switched the ball to his left and scooped it off the backboard for two points. Like Erving's baseline floater, it is one of the most memorable athletic plays in basketball history.

Erving and Jordan were fortunate enough to have lengthy, successful careers. Hawkins played so much of his best ball in small-time pro leagues and with the Harlem Globetrotters that his legs were worn by injury when he finally made it to the NBA. He was still good enough to make first-team all-star in his initial season, play in 4 NBA All-Star Games, and average 20.7 points and 9.1 rebounds in his four full seasons with the Phoenix Suns.

Hawkins is considered basketball's last true legend. There will never be another player about whom it will be said, "You should have seen him," because televised games and nightly sports highlight shows permit us to see every great player hundreds of times.

"I don't have any problem thinking about what I could have done," Hawkins says. "The people who saw me play would tell you the things that Doc did, they'd already seen me do. Because it's not on film, that's not my fault."

ABOVE: A routine two-handed dunk was almost too easy for Julius "Dr. J" Erving, whose style was so exciting he helped force the merger between the ABA and NBA. RIGHT: Unlike many players who can comfortably launch a shot from anywhere on the court, Chicago power forward Dennis Rodman most often needs to dunk the basketball to feel confident he'll make it. The modern game's most productive rebounder, Rodman gets a lot of his points by slamming in balls he claims from the offensive boards.

CHAPTER THREE

The Defensive End

Half of any basketball game is fun to play. The other half is defense. There is little glory to be had when the opposing team has the ball, except that which is achieved through victory. Whether the scheme is a full-court press that demands an exhaustive effort or a zone that requires players to protect only a small area of the floor, those players on defense must be alert, attentive, energetic, and cohesive.

The best defensive teams generally are among those that win most often, which isn't always true of the best offensive teams. In 1994, only three of the top ten highest-scoring teams in college basketball reached the NCAA Tournament. Of the ten best defensive teams, seven made the tournament. The 1981–1982 Denver Nuggets scored more points than any team in NBA history, 126.5 per game, but finished in second place and lost in the first round of the playoffs. In 1954–1955, the Syracuse Nationals allowed their opponents to score just 89.7 points per game, the best defensive performance ever by a pro team. They won the NBA championship.

The teams coached by Mike Krzyzewski at Duke University and Bob Knight at Indiana are best known for their devotion to ruthless, unyielding, man-to-man defense. Other coaches, such as John Chaney of Temple and Nolan Richardson of Arkansas, prefer to rely on zones. In either case, the primary element of defense is players who are willing to work.

"All kids can play good D," says Purdue University coach Gene Keady. "They just don't want to. Some will get to where they want to because they see they can win more often."

An effective defender will have quick feet, an even quicker mind, and enough strength to avoid being pushed around. He will analyze the strengths of the player he is guarding and then force him toward his weaknesses. Defensive players have to do what they can without using their hands extensively; in both college and professional basketball, officials watch closely to see that no offensive player is hand-checked by a defender.

There are moments when a player on defense can be noticed for something other than a personal foul — when he blocks a shot or makes a steal — but defending within the team concept is more important and produces greater results. Keady says his objective is to have all five of his players working to guard the three

LEFT: Alonzo Mourning left college basketball as the all-time leading shot-blocker and is now exercising his specialty for the Miami Heat. Shot-blocking requires agility, extraordinary size or jumping ability, and a keen sense of timing. ABOVE: As a six-foot-nine-inch (205cm) point guard, Magic Johnson liked to keep the ball behind him and use his strength to back down defensive players. Johnson's uncommon size for a point guard forced Golden State to use forward Chris Mullin to defend him.

players who, at any given time, are in the best position on the court to score.

No player has ever proven he can consistently stop the Chicago Bulls' Michael Jordan, but former Detroit Pistons coach Chuck Daly did. He devised a series of defensive maneuvers to be used when the Pistons played the Bulls that were called "The Jordan Rules." If Jordan made a particular move, the Pistons had a collective answer. In 1989 and 1990, Detroit beat Chicago in the Eastern Conference finals and won the NBA title.

For Jordan, those games were among the least pleasurable of his career, although he eventually helped the Bulls to surpass Detroit and go on to win three NBA championships. It may not be fun to play defense, but the best defenders enjoy seeing their opponents bothered.

Don Buse, who played most of his pro career for the Indiana Pacers and specialized in defending opposing point guards, explains as well as anyone why intense defense can be so troublesome to opponents. "Nobody likes to have a guy right up in his face."

The Steal

An admirer of Hall of Fame guard Walt Frazier once praised his uncanny ability to steal the ball by saying, "He could take the hubcaps off a car going fifty miles an hour." A player who dribbled the basketball in Frazier's vicinity was just begging to have it taken away.

You won't find any evidence on Frazier, though. As adept as he was at stealing the basketball, Frazier played six seasons and made the league's all-defensive team five times before the National Basketball Association started keeping a numerical record of his brilliance.

He wasn't as fortunate in that sense as Larry Steele, who practically had this statistical category named in his honor. Steele, a six-foot-five-inch (195cm) swingman who played college basketball at Kentucky, swiped the ball 217 times in his third season, 1973–1974. The first player ever to lead the NBA in steals was named Steele.

"I'm a pretty straightforward guy," Steele said. "I'd have to admit that throughout that year, I probably picked up one or two steals on the road [just] because my name was Steele."

Blessed with quickness and good athletic instincts, Steele developed his defensive skills because he attended a small high school in Indiana and couldn't find consistent one-on-one competition. So he played his buddies one-on-two. "One-on-one was not much of a challenge," he says. "I got to develop the anticipation from playing against two guys. You had to learn to guard both of them. That just carried over into college and the pros."

Austin Carr believes the elimination of hand-checking tactics prior to the 1994–1995 season was the most drastic change in the game since he retired in 1981. "When I played, guys who didn't have the foot speed could still hang around, because they could handcheck," Carr says.

Players are still permitted to use their hands on defense, of course, provided they use them to take away the ball or block an attempted shot. The steal is not as devastating a play as the block, but a lot of blocks wind up rolling over the end line or flying into the seats. A lot of steals wind up as fast-breaks, which can provide a 4-point swing in favor of the team lucky enough to have somebody like six-foot-four-inch (193cm) Jason Kidd, point guard for the Dallas Mavericks.

"The number one thing a steal does is it takes away the possession from the opponent," Steele says, "but the thing that makes it a weapon is it usually results in an easy opportunity at the other end, an excellent opportunity to score. The steals category tells how many you were able to pick up, but the underlying factor is the pressure you were able to put on the other team."

The players who steal the ball most frequently get the majority by stepping between a passer and his intended target, not by swiping them from players who are dribbling. "Jerry West was incredible about playing passing lanes," says Steele, mentioning another Hall of Fame guard who came along before steal statistics were kept. "He could disrupt the entire offense by getting in there and causing trouble, harassing the opponent."

This is why it's impossible to know by looking at a player whether he might be good at stealing the ball. Frazier built his reputation on his ability to undress an opposing ballhandler, but most players who are good at this are best at disrupting the flow of the other team's offense. The NBA steals leaders have ranged in size from six-foot-nine-inch (205cm) Magic Johnson of the Los Angeles Lakers to six-foot-one-inch (185cm) John Stockton of the Utah Jazz, with six-foot-six-inch (198cm) forwards Rick Barry and M.L. Carr in between.

Steals are taken by players who have astonishing speed and quickness, such as 1984 leader Rickey Green of the Utah Jazz and former Philadelphia guard Maurice Cheeks, who retired in 1993 as the league's career leader. Others make steals by using their long arms and sharp anticipation to swipe the ball, like six-foot-seven-inch (200cm) Nate McMillan of the Seattle SuperSonics or former Celtics forward Larry Bird.

A steal can be a matter of teamwork. As a guard for the 1976 Indiana Hoosiers, the last team to win the NCAA championship with an unbeaten record, Quinn Buckner depended on his teammate Bobby Wilkerson's defensive skill when chasing interceptions. "Bobby was such a good defensive player that it allowed me to have the freedom to play the way I could play," Buckner says. "The Lord

OPPOSITE: Boston Celtics rookie Eric Williams goes for a steal against Los Angeles center Vlade Divac.

OPPOSITE: The Spurs' Avery Johnson hustles to cause a turnover against the Philadelphia 76ers. ABOVE: Even big men get a steal here and there. Portland's Buck Williams knocks the ball loose from Karl Malone.

blessed me with the gift to understand the game, so I could read where the ball was going, run, and create traps, and Bobby was there to back it up." Buckner had the same advantage playing alongside Dennis Johnson with the Boston Celtics, and picked up an NBA championship ring in 1984 along with 1,337 career steals.

The steal is a dynamic play, but not always fundamentally sound. Whether the attempt is made by reaching to grab the ball off a dribble or by stepping to intercept a pass, if a productive interceptor like Elliot Perry of the Phoenix Suns is going after a steal, he is moving himself out of proper defensive position. It is a gamble, and the best defenders known when it's a safe bet.

"If you're always trying to steal the basketball, you're going to put your team in jeopardy," Steele says. "Every easy basket you get, you might give up one by trying to make the steal. It's really about judgment."

Shot Rejection

Basketball players tend to take rejection personally. They can grow to handle the disappointment of being cut from a team or traded, but they never get used to seeing one of their shots wind up in the third row of bleachers. The blocked shot is the game's ultimate psychological weapon.

A player who has a ball stolen from him is embarrassed, but the one whose shot is blocked is humiliated. When that player returns with the ball, he is looking for revenge and is no longer thinking clearly. Tree Rollins, whose career with the Atlanta Hawks and Orlando Magic placed him among the five most prolific shot blockers in the history of the NBA, always tried to gain that advantage.

"In my mind as a shot blocker," Rollins says, "once I get him to come at me and make it personal, he's taking the other four guys out of the offense. That guy is going to come back and try to score on just one." And if he is blocked again, he's finished. "It becomes an intimidation factor. Not only does it have a psychological effect on the opposing team, it fires up your guys."

The shot blocker is basketball's strikeout ace. At its core, the block counts as nothing more than a missed shot for the opposing team, but its impact on the game—and on the player who was rejected—is much greater.

Most players will do anything to avoid having their shot rejected, in part because a blocked shot is certainly not going to wind up in the basket, but also to escape that "in-your-face" feeling. This, too, enhances the value of an effective shot blocker. He creates misses by forcing players to alter their shots.

Blocked shots have always existed in basketball, but they weren't counted in the NBA until the 1973–1974 season, and the NCAA didn't start keeping track until 1986. David Robinson won the first college title as a seven-foot-one-inch (215cm) junior for the Naval Academy. He swatted down a record 5.9 shots per game, wiping a dozen possible points per game from the other team's score.

For the best of the erasers, it is less about being able to block a shot one-on-one than about being a threat to everyone on the court. "A shot blocker is [not only] someone who can get the shot from his man, but is [also] the one who can get the shot from so many people," says seven-foot-two-inch Dikembe Mutombo of the Denver Nuggets.

When Rollins played full-time, he would chase after every shot that came in his direction. His coach with the Atlanta Hawks, Hubie Brown, used to tell him, "You've got 6 fouls; don't bring any of them back to the bench." The threat of being called for a foul, though, causes some talented big men to avoid going after blocks. With his size, jumping ability, and intimidating look, seven-foot-one-inch (215cm) Shaquille O'Neal of the Magic should be a tremendous shot blocker. He once got 15 in a game, but annually he ranks behind smaller players like Hakeem Olajuwon of the Houston Rockets and Alonzo Mourning of the Miami Heat. "Anticipation is the thing, thinking where the shooter wants to shoot from and then getting to that spot," Mourning says, indicating that the block is as much about brain as brawn.

Being tall isn't enough. There are lots of players who are close to seven feet (213cm) who aren't effective shot blockers, and plenty who aren't that big who knock down shots with regularity. One of the key ingredients to Mourning's defensive dominance is timing. He knows when to leave his feet to take a shot out of the air, and he recognizes when a player is trying to fake him into jumping.

Rollins, as an assistant coach with the Orlando Magic, has tried to convey that approach to O'Neal. "On offense, he's always focused on where the ball is," Rollins says. "If we can get him to do that defensively, we'll have what everyone wants: a complete basketball player. Shaquille should get at least 2 or 3 more blocks per game,

ABOVE: Although best known for his ability to steal the basketball, Hall of Fame guard Walt Frazier of the New York Knicks was a complete defensive player who could occasionally swat down an opponent's shot. OPPOSITE: Utah forward Karl Malone finds that Orlando Magic center Shaquille O'Neal may not yet be an accomplished shot-blocker, but he's still an intimidating presence because of his size and strength.

but he's not concentrating on it. He tells me every night, 'If I block a shot, I might get a foul.' He's right, but you still can block the shot. Guys are conscious of playing the game, staying in the game, and it's tough to get guys to concentrate on blocks."

Some players try to draw their opponents into traps. Vin Baker of the Milwaukee Bucks says he might offer token resistance on the first attempt, daring the guy with the ball to feel secure. "It's like a challenge. If he tries that again, I may look like I'm sitting back, but no, I'm there, hopefully right on the ball."

Shawn Bradley of the Philadelphia 76ers, who stands seven feet six inches (228cm), gets a lot of his blocks because opponents never get used to the idea that someone could be so tall. They'll take a shot no normal human being could block, then receive a sudden reminder they aren't playing against a normal human. It often works a little like that for six-foot-nine-inch (205cm) Donyell Marshall of the Golden State Warriors. His long arms give him the reach of someone who stands perhaps seven feet one inch (215cm); when players consider only his height in making the instant decision to squeeze off a shot, they can fool themselves into being rejected.

"When I block somebody, that sends a message to anybody else who tries to take it to the hole: don't take me for granted. I'm here," Marshall says. "A block is a powerful thing."

The Rebound

As a Kevin Johnson jumper heads toward the goal, Charles Barkley grows increasingly pessimistic. He has no choice but to assume his teammate's shot will miss. A rebounder expects every shot to clunk off the rim or the backboard, perhaps even his own. If Barkley allows himself to think any other way, the ball will belong to someone else.

"Technique is good, but you can have all the technique in the world and you still have to go get the ball," says Barkley of the Phoenix Suns, one of the most powerful rebounders in NBA history. "That's what it's all about."

The rebound is about turning nothing into something. From still another missed shot can result the outlet pass that ignites a beautifully drilled fast break or a thundering tip-slam that shakes the basket support and the opposing team. Only on occasion is the rebound itself something to see, and even then, the action that leads up to the rebound is likely to include a tangle of arms and legs and the unsettling thud of colliding bodies.

Rebounding is basketball's dirty business. Shooting, passing, dribbling, dunking—each is an act of grace. Rebounding is rugged, demanding, and artless. There is no statistical record, aside from scoring, that will carry a player to wide recognition faster than rebounding, but that does not make it pretty. "A lot of it is effort," says Lon

Portland's Clifford Robinson (opposite) could get this shot away easily against most NBA small forwards, but six-foot-nine-inch (205cm) Donyell Marshall of the Golden State Warriors is a threat because of his extremely long arms. If height were all that mattered, Charlotte's Larry Johnson (top) and Charles Barkley (above) of Phoenix would not be among the NBA's best rebounders. They give up several inches of height to opponents, but rarely give up the ball.

Silas wasn't a great leaper, either, but he has always maintained that most rebounds are taken below the rim. "Paul Silas couldn't jump worth a darn, but he got a lot of rebounds because of how hard he worked at it," says Atlanta Hawks coach Lenny Wilkins. "The guy who moves, the guy who's relentless, gets all the rebounds." Silas proved that even as seven-footers (213cm) became common in the NBA, height wasn't the only ingredient to rebounding. Barkley has continued that tradition. While still a member of the Philadelphia 76ers in 1986-1987, he led the NBA with 14.6 per game. He is a better jumper than Silas, but then, he is only six feet four and a half inches (194cm) tall.

Larry Johnson of the Charlotte Hornets plays power forward at six feet six inches (198cm); it helps that he carries 250 pounds (114kg) of solid muscle. "I'm stronger than most of these other guys. I bring something different," Johnson says. "Some six-foot-ten-inch [208cm] guy can jump out of the gym, but he can't be used to 250 pounds pounding on him like this." Johnson claims to grab most of his rebounds without hardly leaving the floor.

"I was taught at a very young age how to see where the ball would come off the rim," says former Indiana Pacers center Mel Daniels, who stood six feet nine inches (205cm) and led the American Basketball Association in rebounding three times and averaged 14.9 per game during his nine-year pro career. "You have to have an appetite for rebounding, for being aggressive, playing hard; like Charles Barkley saying, 'That's *my* basketball.' It's easy to stand around and watch somebody else get it."

Daniels believes "you have to be a little psychotic" to be a great rebounder. "I think Dennis Rodman is an example of that." Rodman, who plays for the Chicago Bulls, takes a single-minded approach to the game. At Southeastern Oklahoma State, he was twice the top rebounder in the National Association for Intercollegiate Athletics, a collection of small colleges. In his first few years with the Detroit Pistons, Rodman was a proficient rebounder but not extraordinary, averaging 8.9 per game. At that time, he was dedicating himself to being proclaimed one of the great defensive players in the league; he was named defensive player of the year in 1990 and 1991.

It's hard to gain attention without statistical proof of your accomplishments in sports, and Rodman wants attention badly, which may explain why he changes his hair color from blonde to green to purple, pierces various parts of his body, and has tattoos on the rest. As much to get himself noticed as to make his team a champion, Rodman turned his attention to becoming a prominent rebounder

Kruger, head coach at the University of Illinois. In a serious game, no one picks up a respectable number of rebounds by accident.

In the science of rebounding, the second most important skill is being able to determine what direction the ball is likely to bounce if it misses the target. However, the most important ability is being able to stop someone on the other team from getting to that spot first. These are the elements of positioning, and they are essential to rebounding. Paul Silas, who achieved his greatest success in the mid-seventies with the Boston Celtics, ranks as one of the great rebounders in NBA history, with 12,357 in a sixteen-year career. He was so effective at gaining position on rebounds that it never mattered that he stood only six feet ten inches (208cm), sometimes a half-foot (15.2cm) shorter than the players he was beating on the boards.

OPPOSITE: One of the most important aspects of rebounding is gaining good position. Here Golden State Warrior Kevin Willis and New York Knick Anthony Mason battle underneath. ABOVE: Tattooed power forward Dennis Rodman brought his unusual focus on gathering rebounds to the 1995–1996 Chicago Bulls and proved to be the perfect complement to Michael Jordan's offensive capabilites.

ABOVE: Cleveland Cavaliers center Michael Cage has lasted in the NBA for more than a decade, largely because of the strength and timing that make him a superior rebounder. OPPOSITE: Guard Maurice Cheeks of the Philadelphis 76ers knew enough to stay clear when teammate Moses Malone and the Washington Bullets' Rick Mahorn were banging for a loose rebound.

in 1983. "Dennis Rodman is not that great a leaper, but he's constantly studying where the ball is and constantly working on positioning."

Players willing to rebound without complaint can be extremely valuable. NBA veteran Michael Cage has a career rebound average of 8.4, and led the league in 1987–1988 with 13.0 per game as a member of the Los Angeles Clippers. In five consecutive seasons with the Seattle SuperSonics, he averaged more rebounds than points.

After averaging 8.2 rebounds in his first six seasons with the Atlanta Hawks, seven-foot (213cm) power forward Kevin Wills nearly doubled his rebounding to 15.5 per game in 1992. He gave credit to the great Moses Malone, the six-foot-ten-inch (208cm) center who ranks among the NBA's top five career rebounders. Willis said watching Malone play taught him a lot about the techniques and mentality that make a great boardman. He also admitted it helped that Malone left the Hawks that season, which made more rebounds available. When Dennis Rodman went from the Detroit Pistons to the San Antonio Spurs, his rebounding totals stayed about the same. It was seven-foot-one-inch (215cm) teammate David Robinson who had to adjust to grabbing fewer rebounds, although he remained among the NBA's best.

Silas' rebounding theory involves learning how to channel the maximum amount of strength through one part of your body—a hand, hip, or forearm—and use that force to knock the other guy out of the picture. This is markedly different from what young players are most often taught, which is that blocking out on a rebound is primarily a matter of keeping your body between the ball and the opponent.

Daniels had a third approach when the ball was being shot from outside. He wanted to know at all times where his man was. "Make sure you maintain some type of contact with him. And, once you know if the shot's going to be short or long, go after it. If a shot was from the perimeter, I would put my hand on him and nudge him. That's all I'd need, the split second. Blocking out is for shorter shots."

The other part of rebounding is trying to get to the ball when an opponent—a Silas, Rodman, or Larry Johnson—is doing his best to block that path. "It involves pivoting, changing directions, making quick, aggressive moves," says Bob Huggins, coach at the University of Cincinnati. "You've got to get away from the guy trying to block you out."

during the 1991–1992 season, and has led the NBA in that category every season since.

In the early 1960s, it was common for the Boston Celtics' Bill Russell and the Philadelphia Warriors' Wilt Chamberlain to both grab more than 20 rebounds per game, but as shooters grew more accurate and the opposition for rebounds grew taller, the best rebounders in the NBA were usually good for about 14 a night. When Rodman led the NBA with an 18.7 average in '92, it was the highest in the league in twenty years. Like Silas, Rodman, who stands six feet eight inches (203cm), is smaller than most of the people he beats to the ball.

"Most of the better rebounders are guys who don't necessarily jump," says seven-foot-one-inch (215cm) Tree Rollins, who averaged 9.3 boards for the Atlanta Hawks

The Players

When he was playing college basketball at Michigan State, Shawn Respert shot whenever he wanted, from wherever he wanted. He was a shooting guard, and that's what shooting guards do, at least the good ones. One thing college shooting guards who stand shorter than six feet two inches (187cm) do not do is play that position in the NBA. The pros like their shooting guards six feet four inches (193cm) or taller, so they can better defend against others in the league.

So Respert had to make a change. About to make the most demanding transition in his athletic career, from college ball to the NBA, he had to fashion himself into a point guard. "You hear stories; he's a great shooter, a great scorer, but he's not a point guard. He'll never prosper," Respert says. "That's when I told myself I was going to make myself an NBA player. I was in the gym every day."

There are five basic positions on a basketball floor, although some teams vary their lineups according to the personal tastes of a coach or the available personnel on the roster. The point guard, numbered "1" on a coach's play diagram, is the player who advances the ball upcourt and initiates his team's offensive set. The shooting guard (2) works to free himself in the backcourt for scoring opportunities and often specializes in making three-point shots. The small forward (3) takes a similar approach, but concerns himself more with working the baseline area. The power forward (4) uses his bulk to rebound, score inside, and remove some of the defensive pressure from his team's big man. The center (5) is the focus of most offensive systems, setting himself on the inside with his back to the basket and waiting to accept passes that present scoring opportunities.

Positions aren't as restrictive in basketball as in football or baseball. In football, an offensive tackle has to line up in a certain spot or he's no longer an offensive tackle, and if he's too far out of place, his team could be breaking the rules. A shortstop in baseball can stand anywhere he wants on defense, but if he's not somewhere between second base and third, there'll be a large gap in his team's defense.

FAR LEFT: Patrick Ewing grew from a defensive force as a college player to one of the NBA's most dangerous offensive centers and a fixture with the New York Knicks. LEFT, TOP: Before joining the Milwaukee Bucks, Shawn Respert developed the passing skills necessary to make him fit in at point guard among the professionals. LEFT, BOTTOM: Lean and agile instead of big and muscular, Robert Horry of the world champion Houston Rockets is helping to redefine the power forward position in the NBA.

When he entered the NBA, Atlanta's Steve Smith was expected to be an excellent scorer because of his height, shooting stroke, and dexterity, but he quickly showed that his command of the game was strong enough that he could also play point guard.

The five positions in basketball evolved from the original guards, forwards, and center as players became more specialized and were recognized for their abilities in certain areas. It was necessary to have someone help the center in rebounding, so teams tended to use one bigger player at forward, creating the position of power forward. It was found helpful to have a single player in charge of setting up the offense, which led to the birth of the point guard.

Players are often capable of playing one or more positions. Robert Horry of the Houston Rockets was drafted as a small forward, and played that position when his team won the 1993 NBA championship. When the team traded top rebounder Otis Thorpe the following season, Horry was switched to power forward. Steve Smith of the At-

lanta Hawks has played shooting guard and point guard. In the 1980 NBA Finals, Magic Johnson played the point for the first 5 games, then took over at center for Game Six when seven-foot–two-inch (218cm) Kareem Abdul-Jabbar was injured. Johnson scored 42 points, grabbed 15 rebounds, and passed for 7 assists as the Lakers clinched the first of five championships with Magic as their leader.

For a basketball player, the position presents a list of requirements, but should not be taken as a series of restrictions. Each spot on the floor mandates certain talents, first and foremost the ability to play defense and prevent the other team's power forward or shooting guard from fulfilling his duties. If a player is too concerned about what position he plays, however, he may neglect other possible contributions he can make to his team. A shooting guard who thinks only of shooting may keep his job, but he probably won't improve his team.

"I grew up considering myself a player, and I would play with whoever was on the court," says Quinn Bucker, ostensibly a point guard for the 1976 NCAA champions at Indiana and 1984 NBA champion Celtics. "If there were aspects of the game that I felt I could do better on the team than anyone else, I would take those on, including scoring. If I felt I had to be more of a scorer, I would have taken that on. I felt if I played forward, I could affect the outcome of the game."

The Point Guard

When it is time for Anfernee "Penny" Hardaway to fire a jump shot, race through the lane for a layup, or make a no-look pass that gives center Shaquille O'Neal an easy slam, he simply knows it. Hardaway calls it instinct, but everything he does in a basketball game is filtered through knowledge he gained by running his team in high school, at the University of Memphis, and with the Orlando Magic.

There are players who are born to be point guards, but no one is a point guard at birth. There is too much to know. There is ballhandling, passing, shooting, play-calling, and reacting to defensive pressure and tactics. The point guard must recognize the proper moment to take advantage of his skills or his teammates' and keep constant track of the score and the time remaining in the game.

"I just try to bring leadership, really," Hardaway says. "If I'm out there messing up, then everybody else is going to mess up. As a leader, I'm trying to instill confidence in my teammates. Everything runs from the point guard. He's the head of the body."

The point guard is director and conductor, engineer and pilot, chairman and CEO. And, occasionally, psychologist. He infuses a team with creative energy and drives the other players in the pursuit of victory, following whatever route seems prudent. All that does or doesn't work

No one has passed for more assists in the five-decade history of the NBA than Utah Jazz guard John Stockton, who broke the career record set by Magic Johnson. However, he would not be a complete point guard without the ability to consistently beat his man to the basket and score in traffic. Adding his own baskets to those produced by his assists, Stockton directly accounts for 36 points in a typical game.

is his responsibility; the point guard has control not only of his team's offense, but also its defense. There has never been a basketball player who does not enjoy seeing his shot fall through the basket, and if a teammate is frustrated, the point guard can energize that player by passing him the ball or calling his play, making him feel a part of things. There have been teams that won NCAA or NBA championships without great small forwards or even centers, but rare is the team that wins it all without superior play at the point.

"Basically," says Nick Van Exel of the Los Angeles Lakers, "the point guard is the man."

There is no room for selfishness in a point guard. In fact, the statistic by which players at the position are measured, the assist, is an accounting of how often and effectively they share the ball with teammates. An assist is awarded when a pass leads directly to a basket. John Stockton, point guard for the Utah Jazz, is the only player in the history of the National Basketball Association who has recorded 10,000 assists—that's 20,000 points he produced for the Jazz.

After he finished his stint at Gonzaga University in Spokane, Washington, Stockton surprised a lot of basketball followers by nearly making the 1984 U.S. Olympic team, which featured Michael Jordan, Patrick Ewing, and Chris Mullin, and was considered one of the best teams of college players ever assembled. Stockton then surprised himself by becoming a first-rate NBA player after he was drafted by the Jazz as the sixteenth pick in the 1984 first round. He never saw himself as having the physical ability to compete with the world's best players.

"He's always doubted himself, so he worked hard to prove himself. That doubt was a plus for him," says Los Angeles Lakers superstar Magic Johnson. "He's by far the best floor leader there is. There's nobody that can distribute the ball, plus lead his team, like John Stockton."

There are creative point guards, scoring point guards, and point guards who are extraordinary leaders. If a player has just one of these attributes, he can succeed at the position. Stockton is an enduring all-star because he combines all of these qualities. Hardaway is an emerging all-star—and Johnson is headed toward the Basketball Hall of Fame—for the same reason.

For a point guard, creativity is the ability to generate a play with only a smidgen of help from his teammates, or none at all. Bob Cousy, who led the Boston Celtics to six NBA championships from 1957 to 1963, was perhaps the first great playmaker in basketball. His passing and ball-handling skills revolutionized the game and made other small players realize what they could accomplish. Only six feet one inch (185cm) tall, Cousy excelled at driving past the backcourt defense and slipping the ball to a forward for an unguarded layup. He led the NBA in assists eight times and once passed for 19 in a half, a league record.

OPPOSITE: Jason Kidd goes in for an uncontested dunk versus the Knicks. ABOVE: Tiny Charlotte point guard Muggsy Bogues sneaked in between Chicago's Steve Kerr and Michael Jordan, but couldn't prevent the Hornets' first-round playoff loss in 1995.

Creativity is the most elusive of point guard skills, involving the gift of dribbling the ball through narrow cracks in the defense and recognizing passing lanes almost before they develop. It is the one element of the position that truly must come naturally. Kenny Anderson of the New Jersey Nets has it. Van Exel, who comes by his success through scoring and leadership, does not. The creative point guard may not be the one most likely to beat you, but he is the one who is guaranteed to dazzle you.

From the time he was in ninth grade at Archbishop Molloy High School in Queens, New York City, Anderson was conjuring passes that his teammates often did not expect, and that fans could hardly believe. He needed only two years at Georgia Tech University before he was ready for the NBA. Because Hardaway demonstrated the talent, his coaches kept him at point guard even after he grew to be six feet five inches (195cm) in tenth grade.

"I was the tallest guy on the team, and they put me at the point guard spot," Hardaway says. "My high school basketball coach knew that I had the skills to be a point guard. If he would have been like the other coaches, thinking, 'You're six-five and you need to be in the post,' my game would have been totally different." Hardaway always had the physical gifts to play the position, but has had to learn to be a leader. His coaches in college and high school often chastised him for not shooting enough; even when his team needed him to score, Hardaway preferred to pass the ball and make his teammates happy.

Most point guards are the smallest players on their team, from the extreme case of five-foot-three-inch (160cm) Tyrone Bogues of the Charlotte Hornets to more standard compact models like six-foot (183cm) Tim Hardaway of the Miami Heat and Mark Price of the Washington Bullets, and six-foot-one-inch (185cm) Kevin Johnson of the Phoenix Suns. Their skill at shooting from the outside and changing directions in traffic places them among the best point guards.

Penny Hardaway is among a select breed of point guards, bringing size to the position along with talent. Hardaway's height enables him to see over smaller defenders, and sometimes to pass over their heads, giving him one more avenue to a perfect assist than is enjoyed by a six-foot-one-inch (185cm) or six-foot-two-inch (187cm) player. Jason Kidd of the Dallas Mavericks, at six feet four inches (193cm), has that advantage along with tremendous strength packed inside his 210-pound (95.5kg) frame. After just two seasons at the University of California, Kidd tied with Detroit forward Grant Hill for NBA rookie of the year honors in 1995.

The pioneer among big point guards was Magic Johnson, who stood six feet nine inches (205cm), weighed 225 pounds (102kg) and was gifted enough to have been an all-star at any position on the court. No one before or since could rival his ability to handle the ball, pass, and direct his team, all while standing nearly a foot taller than many of those matched against him.

Johnson was named most valuable player for the regular season and for the NBA Finals three times each. His greatest talent was in gaining an understanding of his teammates—whether it was forward Greg Kelser running the break as the two led Michigan State to the 1979 NCAA title, or Laker teammate James Worthy's knack for scoring on mid-range jumpers—and making sure those players became as productive as possible. "Lots of guys can run an offense," Johnson once said. "The hard thing is to get the ball to a player at his spot, a place he can score from."

Sacramento's Tyus Edney is as quick as any pro point guard, but veteran lefty Kenny Anderson needs only the slightest misstep from an opponent to leave him behind and penetrate the lane.

Considered by many to be the greatest small man to play basketball, Isiah Thomas operated so smoothly on the court, it sometimes seemed his feet never touched the floor. Thomas, who led the Detroit Pistons to two NBA championships, was never needlessly flashy, but still could dazzle the crowd when he sensed it would pay off.

Phil Ford, twice an All-American at North Carolina and considered by many to be the greatest college point guard, believes scoring should never be a point guard's personal objective. And yet he stands ahead of such great players as Michael Jordan, James Worthy, Charlie Scott, and Billy Cunningham as the leading scorer in Tar Heels history. Ford shot 53 percent from the field and averaged 18.6 points per game in his four seasons (1974–1978) as a starter, then went on to become the NBA's rookie of the year in 1979.

"I think a point guard's mentality should be that his job is to try to get his team to get the ball in the basket, and he doesn't care who does it, doesn't care how it's done, as long as it's legal," Ford says. "I think there's a difference between a point guard that can score and a scoring point guard. It's not that I looked for my shot, but if the shot was there, I'd take it. I really did not care about scoring....It's just something that happened."

It worked that way for Walt Frazier, who led the New York Knicks to two NBA championships in the early 1970s. He is the greatest defensive point guard ever, making the NBA's all-defensive team in seven consecutive seasons from 1969 to 1975, and he played with such productive scorers as forward Bill Bradley, center Willis Reed, and shooting guard Earl Monroe. And still, because he was so skilled at

Phil Ford controlled the basketball so well for North Carolina, Coach Dean Smith devised the controversial "four-corners" slowdown offense to put opponents at his mercy. It helped get the Tar Heels to the 1977 NCAA title game, but Marquette won the championship.

controlling the flow of the game, Frazier was able to score 18.9 points per game during his career.

Hall of Famers Nate "Tiny" Archibald and Dave Bing did not always have talented teammates, so they often had to look to score themselves. That led to Archibald producing perhaps the greatest offensive season ever for a point guard: 34 points and 11.4 assists per game for the Kansas City/Omaha Kings in 1972–1973, the first time any player had led the NBA in both categories. Bing averaged 20.3 points and 6.0 assists in twelve seasons, mostly with the Detroit Pistons. Their styles were similar to that of twelve-time all-star Isiah Thomas, who retired from the Pistons in 1994 with career averages of 19.2 points and 9.3 assists per game. Thomas had such great quickness that he could break down a defense by driving into the lane for a layup or pass, and he was a prolific outside shooter, with 398 career three-pointers.

Thomas was also a tremendous leader, infusing the kind of confidence in his teammates that Van Exel does with the Lakers today and Corey Beck did with the Arkansas Razorbacks when they won the NCAA title in 1994. Thomas was the point guard for an NCAA champion (Indiana, 1981) and two NBA champs (Detroit, 1989 and 1990), and he was named most valuable player in two of those three playoffs.

"You've got to bring a lot of energy, a lot of enthusiasm," says Van Exel, who took the University of Cincinnati to the NCAA Final Four in 1992, after an absence of nearly thirty years. "You've got to go out there and run the show, let everybody know you're in control, handle your business on the court and off the court."

"Once everybody has a bond, everybody believes totally in their point guard, they feel more comfortable," Beck says. "I think it's real important that the other players believe in you."

The Shooting Guard

He couldn't do much with a curveball, but Michael Jordan always could hit a jump shot. He wasn't bad at stealing bases, but it was nothing like the way he steals a basketball on defense and slams it through the goal at the opposite end of the court.

Jordan, considered by many to be the greatest player in all of basketball history thus far, accomplished so much with such apparent ease on behalf of the Chicago Bulls that he grew to miss the challenge he once found in sports and decided, in 1994, to try his hand at another. He joined the Chicago White Sox organization, spent a year batting .202 with the Class AA Birmingham Barons, and then came to miss the sport that had been so much a part of his life.

"I tried to stay away as much as I could, but when you love something so long and and you walk away from it, you can only stay away so long," Jordan said. "I missed my friends and teammates."

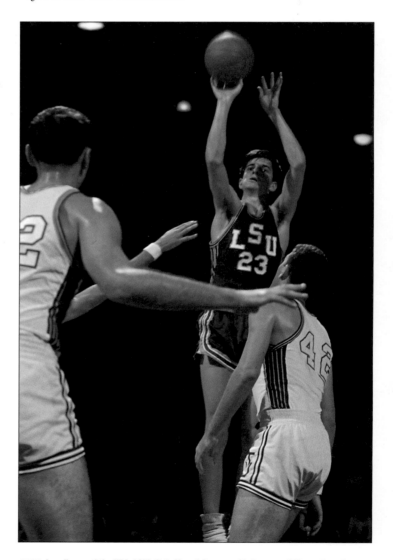

ABOVE: In college and the NBA, LSU's Pete Maravich was unable to connect his great scoring ability to team success. OPPOSITE: Michael Jordan often doesn't decide exactly what he is going to do until he leaves his feet. Here he looks to shoot against the Portland Trail Blazers.

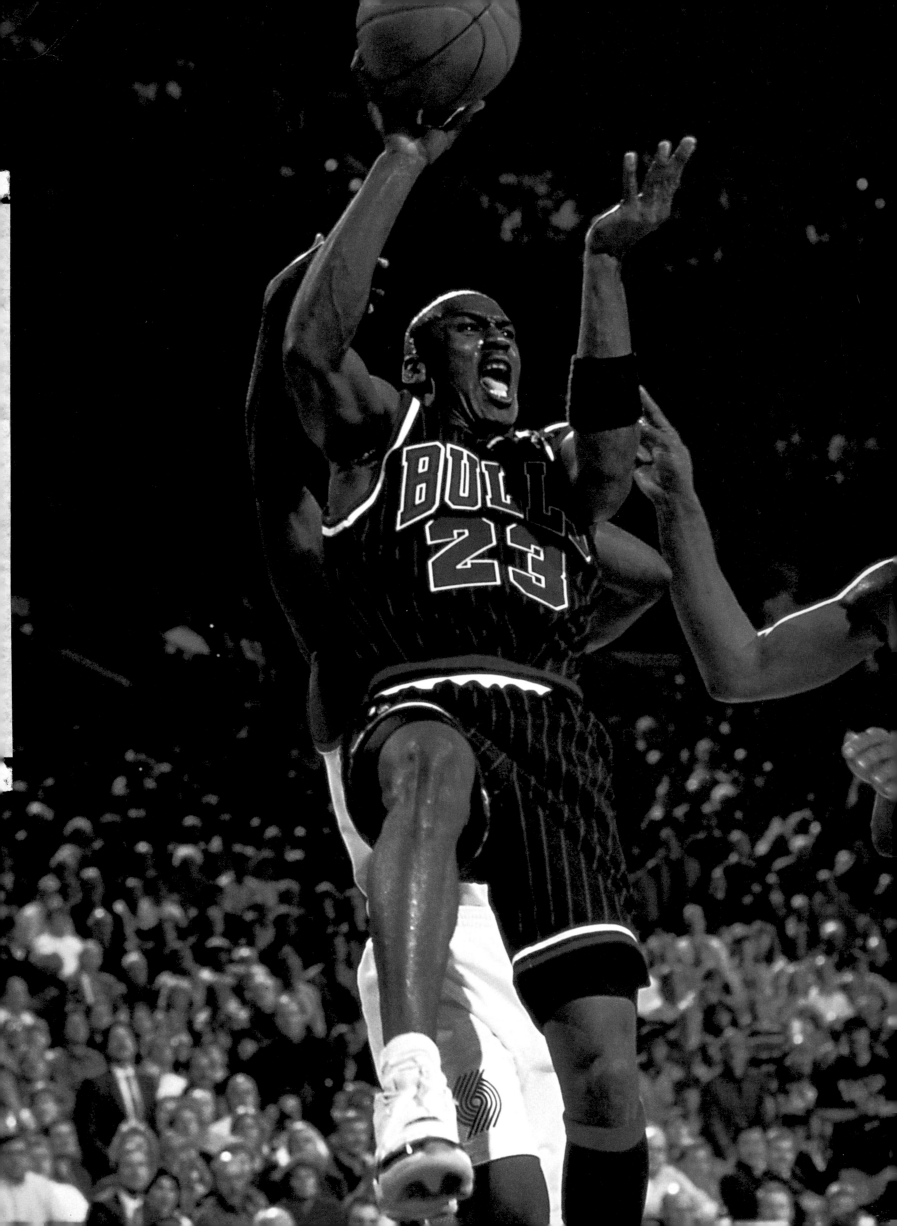

Jordan won the league scoring championship in seven of his first nine seasons, has compiled the highest career scoring average of any player, and a shooting percentage of nearly .520. He has been named Most Valuable Player three times and led the Bulls to three consecutive NBA titles, making them only the third team in history to record that achievement.

Jordan is able to jump better than most players, but what separates him is his astonishing body control. He can contort his body to alter his flight after he has gone airborne. Although his ballhandling skill is often overlooked, he dribbles the ball and passes well enough to play point guard, which he has done for the Bulls when they've needed direction on offense. He developed himself into a consistent outside shooter with the range to make three-pointers.

If there is any position in basketball from which it is difficult to dominate the game, it is the position of shooting guard. This should make Jordan's impact on the game all the more amazing. The shooting guard has the license to fire on offense, or else he wouldn't be filling that position, but otherwise he is required to perform fewer duties. He is welcome to help with rebounding, with passing to the open man, and of course he must cover his man on defense, but a shooting guard with no other offensive talent than shooting can still last a while.

There have been a handful of shooting guards, in addition to Jordan, who could do anything you asked of them and do it better than nearly everyone who has played the game. Oscar Robertson of the Cincinnati Royals and Milwaukee Bucks was the most versatile big guard to play in the NBA. At six feet five inches (195cm) and 220 pounds (100kg), he had the muscle to score inside and grab rebounds, the jump shot to get baskets from the outside, and mesmerizing passing ability. In 1962, he became the only player ever to average a triple double—double-figure totals in points, rebounds, and assists—for an entire season. As a college player at the University of

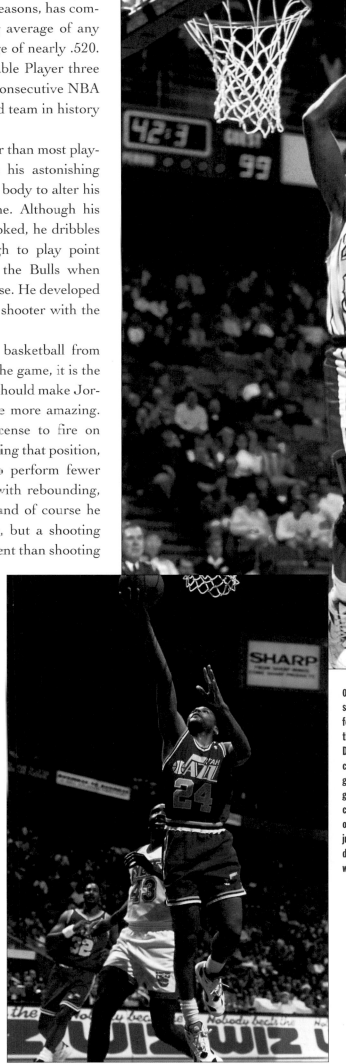

OPPOSITE: Toronto forward John Salley is merely a spectator as Indiana guard Reggie Miller, widely feared for his long-range shooting skills, squeezes through the defense for a tough layup. ABOVE: Dunking was about all anyone thought Clyde Drexler could do as he left college, but he developed his game to become one of the great pro shooting guards and lead the Houston Rockets to an NBA championship in 1995. LEFT: Guard Jeff Malone was one of the NBA's prolific scoring machines, launching jumpers with his ultra-quick release before defenders could react and outmuscling those who challenged his control of the lane.

THE SEARCH FOR TALENT

There will be more than forty thousand spectators collected under the RCA Dome when the 1997 NCAA Final Four is contested in Indianapolis. When some of the key players for those teams were discovered, at the 1993 Nike All-American Camp, the audience in the RCA Dome numbered closer to four hundred.

The Nike Camp is an annual event sponsored by the athletic apparel company in which 130 of the top high school prospects are collected for five days of top-level competition and instruction on academic and social skills. The players get the opportunity to prove themselves against highly regarded athletes from other areas of the country, with coaches from every big-time college basketball program gathered in the stands.

Most players who wind up in college basketball participate in camps and tournaments each July, where coaches are permitted to spend the month evaluating prospects. Those summer events are important, because college coaches are only allowed to watch prospects play a couple of times during the regular season. The Nike Camp tries to concentrate the finest players in one place for one week.

"I think you have to look at this place as the ultimate for talent evaluation," says Bob Gibbons, who runs a scouting service ranking the best high school players all around the U.S. to which college teams and college fans subscribe.

For the colleges, maybe Gibbons is right. The pros have their own versions of the Nike Camp, though, and the players are even better there. Most who wind up playing professional basketball compete in one or all of the three spring events that follow the college season: the Portsmouth Invitational, the Desert Classic in Phoenix, and the NBA

Pre-Draft Camp in Chicago. The idea in all cases is to gather the most talented players together and see who stands out, based on individual skills and the ability to mesh quickly with teammates.

Finding the best college players for the pro tryout camps is the job of Marty Blake, director of the NBA Scouting Service. Gibbons does the same for the Nike Camp. They earn their living by recognizing basketball talent in all its forms, from the energetic point guard to the hyperactive small forward. It is an imprecise science, and mastery is rare.

Whereas the Chicago Pre-Draft camp is only open to pro scouts and reporters, the Nike Camp is open to the public, and admission is free, but fans have never demonstrated much interest in attending. The teams are constructed merely to make them as competitive as possible, with little attention to geography. So there is no rooting interest. Few in the public have come to understand that discovering a player can be one of basketball's quiet joys.

Josh Pastner, who played high school basketball in the Houston area, learned when he was fifteen how thrilling this can be. He watched a player named Tyrone Manlove, a guard from Oregon, score 50 points in a summer all-star tournament. "I just wanted to tell everybody about him." Pastner began sending reports on players to scouting services and continued even as he became a star player himself. When he was spending his summer weeks at camps and tournaments watching for other players in his free time, "All the other kids would go to the mall."

It's likely no one in college basketball spends more time and energy hunting for players than Kevin O'Neill, head coach at the University of Tennessee. When the July evaluation period begins for coaches, he leaves home and does not return until it is finished. "You have ideas on guys when you come in," O'Neill said of his experience watching players in camps, "but you get the chance to measure them against this level of talent. The bottom line is, I've got to like the kid because I'm the one who has to put him in the game."

When players are placed in such large groups and made to compete against each other, those scouting them are sometimes torn. If the players they like do well, other teams may develop interest. If the player does not, he might not be worth worrying about. "I want to see him play well," O'Neill says, "because those are the kids he's going to have to beat the next four years."

When scouts looking for the next great basketball players talk amongst themselves, and scouts generally are the type of people who can't help but talk about the game, they have only two real choices. They can whisper to a trusted colleague what they really think about a player. Or they can lie.

If a coach from St. John's tells another from North Carolina State how desperately he wants to recruit a prospect, it's hard for that N.C. State coach not to want him too. If a general manager for one NBA team makes it plain he plans to draft a six-foot-ten-inch (208cm) power forward from Oklahoma State, that player might be more attractive to some teams with earlier draft picks.

With a strong performance at the Desert Classic in Phoenix, former Iowa State center Loren Meyer established himself as a first-round draft choice and was chosen by the Dallas Mavericks.

Elden Campbell was considered to be soft and lazy as a college player, but Los Angeles GM Jerry West coveted his skills.

So scouting is primarily about trying to keep secrets in an industry where there are so few. There aren't many unknown players in high school who are fit prospects for big-time college basketball, and there are fewer playing in college likely to be surprise stars in the pros.

The term "sleeper" is a relic from an era in which professional scouting wasn't as sophisticated as it is today, with each team employing an average of three scouts in addition to the general manager and director of player personnel. Players deemed to be prospects are evaluated as many times as possible during the course of their college careers; often, scouts will see the same player twenty times in person before he enters the draft, and more often on television.

In the strictest sense, Dennis Rodman, the NBA's most proficient rebounder in the 1990s, might have been the last of the sleepers. He was hardly noticed when the Detroit Pistons chose him with the twenty-seventh pick of the 1986 draft after he averaged 24.4 points and 17.8 rebounds per game at Southeastern Oklahoma State, a school that does not compete in the NCAA. It quickly became apparent, as Rodman played superior defense on such great players as Larry Bird of the Boston Celtics and James Worthy of the Los Angeles Lakers, that a lot of people had managed not to notice a very special player.

It still happens that players are missed, but they're usually well-known college players whom scouts don't believe will make the transition to the NBA. Los Angeles Lakers general manager Jerry West has built a championship contender out of such players. Center Vlade Divac, forward Elden Campbell, guards Nick Van Exel and Eddie Jones—none was

Nick Van Exel was a second-round steal for the Lakers.

among the top nine selections in his draft class. West notices potential on other teams, also, which is another important element of scouting. West traded for forward Cedric Ceballos, who became an all-star his first season with the Lakers. Ceballos had a lot in common with his new teammates: he wasn't chosen until the second round, when the Suns took him with the forty-eighth selection.

"I wasn't expecting to be drafted at all," Ceballos says. "I figured I'm here, let's see what I can do. I just tried to learn and keep my mouth shut and watch. I kept the fire of basketball in me, and that's a very important thing, especially if you're at the bottom." Ceballos didn't stay there very long.

Joe Dumars puts up a shot between Seattle's Gary Payton and Shawn Kemp. In 1992–1993 Dumars was seventh in the league in points, averaging 23.5 per game.

When Andrew Toney played shooting guard for the Philadelphia 76ers, he so haunted the Boston Celtics that they traded for defensive specialist Dennis Johnson in order to have some chance of stopping him from scoring.

Cincinnati, he led the NCAA in scoring for three consecutive seasons.

In Robertson's era, only Jerry West of the Los Angeles Lakers could challenge his supremacy. West wasn't as tall, standing six feet two inches (187cm), but his jump shot was an artistic triumph. He wasn't strictly a long-distance operator. He was an excellent passer, and he had a knack for forcing defenders to foul him. He twice led the NBA in free throws attempted, beating out seven-foot-one-inch (215cm) Wilt Chamberlain.

The only other player to lead the NCAA in scoring for three consecutive seasons was Pistol Pete Maravich, who became the all-time scoring leader in college basketball by averaging 44.2 points per game in three seasons at LSU. Maravich could do most anything he wanted with a basketball, equally accomplished at shooting, passing, and

ballhandling, but not limited by convention in any of those skills. He played with style and flash that was not always appreciated in the NBA, although he led the league in scoring with a 31.1 average in 1977 and five times was selected to the All-Star Game.

Not everyone in basketball can agree on what to call the player at this position. Some call it "two-guard," because that is the player's numerical designation when diagraming a play. "Second guard" is used less often, but for the same reason. Others call it "off guard" because the player is considered to play off the ball, waiting for the point guard to initiate the offense. "Wing guard" describes where the

OPPOSITE: Despite a left knee that bothered him through much of his career, Milwaukee shooting guard Sidney Moncrief had enough life in his legs to slash toward the basket ahead of Detroit Pistons guard Vinnie Johnson.

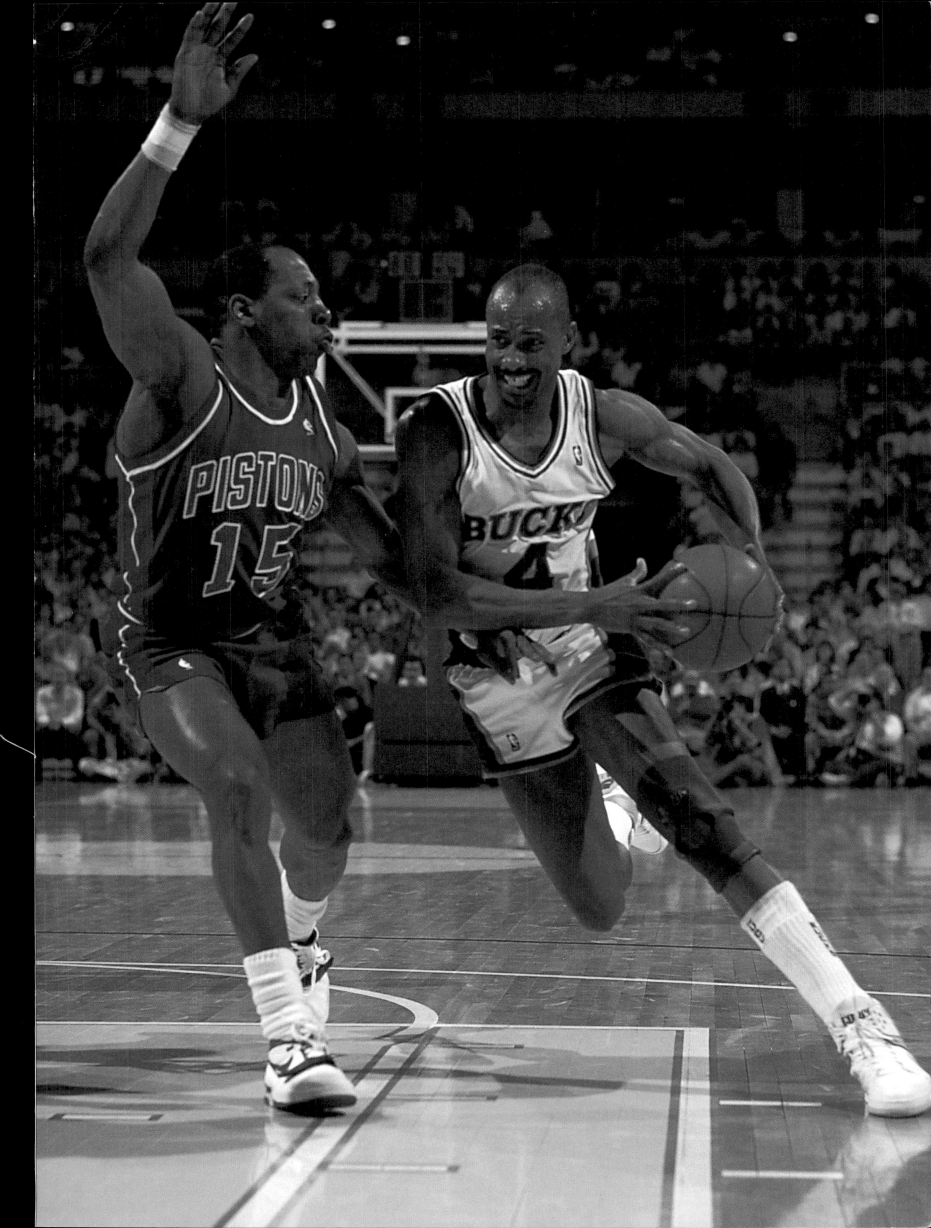

player positions himself on offense, but has slowly faded from use. The people who don't like the term "shooting guard" complain that it implies the player does nothing else, and that others on the court aren't entitled to shoot.

Indeed, there are shooting guards who aren't exceptional shooters, although it's as challenging for them to succeed at basketball's highest levels as it is for wide receivers in football who don't have great speed. They must have some other special talent. Earl "The Pearl" Monroe, a Hall-of-Famer who starred on the New York Knicks' 1973 NBA championship team, was better at breaking down his defender and driving into the lane than firing from long distance. Clyde Drexler of the 1995 champion Houston Rockets is a high-flying acrobat, an inexorable force on the fast break. Sidney Moncrief, a perennial all-star with the Milwaukee Bucks in the 1980s, was perhaps the best defender to play shooting guard, excelling at forbidding the great shooters on opposing teams to do their damage.

With Jordan, Robertson, Maravich, and West as glaring exceptions, shooting guards generally are among the least versatile players on the court; they are required to score and defend, but many are not accomplished passers or ballhandlers. Some of those who played only one note could play it loudly, though. Among those who played the position are the most explosive, focused scorers in the game's history. Andrew Toney had a brief run with the Philadelphia 76ers creating misery for the Boston Celtics; he specialized in firing quickly off the dribble, before the defense could react, and was a key ingredient in the Sixers' 1983 championship. World B. Free—who changed his first name from Lloyd to draw more attention to himself—used his vast shooting range to score 17,955 career points. Jeff Malone, who averaged nearly 20 points per game with the Washington Bullets and Utah Jazz, could back down almost any defender with his strength and sting him with an instantaneous jump shot.

"Shooting was something that I worked on, and I had to," says Ron Boone, who scored 17,437 points in a thirteen-year career divided between the ABA and NBA. He stood only six feet two inches (187cm), but weighed 200 pounds (91kg) and was a powerful player. "In college, I played some forward and even center because of my strength and jumping ability. The fact I played those inside spots, with my back to the basket, I played bigger than most guards my size.

"I was one of those guys who liked to penetrate, and that was my first option early in my career. After I worked hard at shooting my outside jump shot, I felt like that made me a complete player."

The shooting guard has to be inventive in a different manner from the point guard. Whereas the player at the point has to devise ways to defeat the entire defense, the shooting guard focuses mainly on beating his man. He must have moves that trick the defense or bear such force

OPPOSITE: A shooting guard is most valuable when he is putting pressure on the defense. Here, Dallas guard Jimmy Jackson draws the attention of Orlando point guard Penny Hardaway and power forward Horace Grant. ABOVE: Hall of Famer George Gervin used his special finger-roll move to score baskets over smaller guards who couldn't cope with his six-foot-eight-inch (203cm) frame.

that even the well-prepared defender can't help but surrender a basket. "At my position, the two guard, you've got to come back with something new every year," says Jimmy Jackson, a young star with the Dallas Mavericks.

"You have to work on your game all the time. It's just as important now as it was coming through high school and through college. Even though you're at a certain level in the NBA, you can always improve. I think the day you stop improving is the day you need to call it quits."

Jackson stands six feet six inches (198cm) tall, and might have been a small forward just a generation earlier. He developed the necessary ballhandling and passing skills to get by in the backcourt early in his career. "It happened in the seventh grade that our point guard got hurt, so I had to play there. From then on, I really got into passing the ball, shooting the ball, handling the ball, and that just carried on all through high school and through college."

It became important through the 1970s for shooting guards to be taller than they had been in the past. Such players as six-foot-eight-inch (203cm) George Gervin of the San Antonio Spurs and six-foot-seven-inch (200cm) Doug Collins of the Philadelphia 76ers made it difficult for players in the six-foot (183cm) neighborhood to defend at the position. It became unusual to see a point-guard-sized shooting guard in the NBA, but six-foot-two-inch (187cm) Joe Dumars not only became a frequent all-star, he did it by playing defense as well as any player of his era.

Reggie Miller of the Indiana Pacers has the same size advantage, and a volatile on-court personality. He carries on dialogues during games with such courtside fans as film director Spike Lee, who has front row, midcourt season tickets for New York Knicks games at Madison Square Garden. He has become one of the most frequently jeered players as a result. What makes Miller a special player, though, is a shooting range as expansive as any player could imagine. He was almost insulted when the NBA decided to move its three-point line from nearly twenty-four feet (7.3m) to just over twenty-one feet (6.4m). He liked the idea that the three-pointer was a man's shot, his shot. "That was my shot. Now, it's a gimme."

The Small Forward

If the greatest athletes in the sporting world are basketball players, the greatest athletes in the basketball world are small forwards. They aren't always small—Larry Bird is six feet nine inches (215cm), and Danny Manning of the Phoenix Suns is six feet eleven inches (210cm)—but the position includes such a variety of duties that they almost always need to be versatile.

"To be the small forward, you have to be the best athlete on the floor," says the Los Angeles Lakers' Cedric Ceballos. "You have to run constantly. Big men, they go paint to paint. Guards go free throw line to free throw line. Forwards have to go from baseline to baseline and cover every aspect of the court. There's been so many great player at the position, and all of them have had a lot of different talents."

The small forward is the link that binds a basketball offense. If he is a capable passer, he can aid in moving the ball from the backcourt to the post. If he is a mesmerizing passer, such as Bird or the Golden State Warriors' Chris Mullin, he can disable an opponent by presenting such a wide range of possibilities for the defense to consider. If he is neither, a team can drift apart, still aiming for the same goal, the basket, but ambling toward that goal in different directions.

Just as there are certain positions in baseball (third base, first base) where the nature of the game dictates a player must display power in order to be considered an asset, basketball teams must get scoring from their small forwards. John Havlicek of the Boston Celtics in the 1960s and '70s and Scottie Pippen of the 1990s Chicago Bulls scored thousands of points by outrunning opponents and filling lanes on the break, and each displayed a gift for using their own defense to create those opportunities. Alex

WHO NEEDS COLLEGE?

In the *Official NBA Basketball Encyclopedia*, where the records of every player who has appeared in the NBA or ABA are listed, you will find this notation on the same line as Moses Malone's height, weight, and birthday: College—None.

Malone, a six-foot-ten-inch (208cm), 255-pound (116kg) center who dominated high school basketball as few before him, did not need college basketball to prepare himself for the professional game. He signed a letter of intent to attend Maryland, but then was drafted and signed by the ABA's Utah Stars after graduating from Petersburg High in Virginia. He went on to become one of the greatest scorers and rebounders to play in the NBA, and was the league's Most Valuable Player in 1979, 1982, and 1983.

Only twenty-five other players, among the thousands of athletes who have played in the NBA, never attended college. All but nine of those men entered the league before 1950, and most left as quickly as they arrived. Even with the proper preparation, competing in professional basketball is hard enough. Kevin Garnett, who became the fifth pick in the 1995 NBA Draft despite never having played beyond high school, is the latest to try to prove that history can be defeated.

Darryl Dawkins' lack of a college education didn't keep him from being a creative personality, nicknaming himself "Chocolate Thunder" and claiming to be from the planet Lovetron.

High school star Kevin Garnett was introduced to NBA commissioner David Stern just five picks into the 1995 draft.

A six-foot-eleven-inch (210cm) center at Farragut Academy in Chicago, Garnett was not academically eligible to compete in major-college basketball as a freshman, and thus chose to enter the draft. An explosive bundle of energy on the court, Garnett can shoot, pass, and dribble so well that he will play small forward in the pros. Clearly he loves the game, but it's also a business in the NBA. "I always have fun when I play," Garnett says. "I don't go out there and try to do something I know I can't do. I just go out there, be Kevin, and do the things that got me here. Play hard, have fun, smile. That's it.

"If it's serious and there's people paying good money to see you play, I think you should play hard. That's how I was taught coming up, to play hard and give it your all."

Only two players before Garnett declared themselves eligible for the NBA draft directly after finishing high school: six-foot-seven-inch (200cm) forward Bill Willoughby of Englewood, New Jersey, and six-foot-eleven-inch (210cm) center Darryl Dawkins of Orlando, Florida, both in 1975. The difficulty they had in establishing successful careers convinced scores of talented high school players in the two-decade interim to head to college first.

Dawkins never liked to hear suggestions his career was damaged because he didn't play in college, but he never made an all-star team, never averaged 17 points a game, and only five times in fourteen years did he play a full season's worth of games. Willoughby stuck around for eight years and only once played a full season, did not average as much as 8 points per game, and was out of the league by the time he was twenty-seven. He wondered what he might have been like as a pro with some college ball in his background.

A lot of basketball players grow up fast, which is how they come to be basketball players. Maturing is another matter. Competing in the NBA, with its eighty-two-game season (plus exhibitions and playoffs) and rigorous travel schedule, puts a great deal of physical and mental strain on a player. At the same time, playing just three hours a night and practicing for shorter periods on off days leaves a guy like Garnett with more free time than he's accustomed to. And there is the money.

Dawkins thought he jumped into a lot of money when he was drafted by the Philadelphia 76ers in 1975, signing a seven-year contract for one million dollars. Garnett makes three times that much in one year. Keeping track of such riches is often too much for veteran players, many of whom have been burned by callous or unscrupulous agents. How is a teenager to cope?

"I hate to see any kid pass on the opportunity to attend college," says ESPN television basketball analyst Dick Vitale. "The bottom line is that any young man should get the chance to develop as a young man."

Since forward Spencer Haywood of the University of Detroit successfully fought for the right to enter pro basketball without finishing college—he became a five-time all-star with the Seattle SuperSonics and five other teams—hundreds of players have decided to enter the draft before their NCAA eligibility was completed. Most of the players taken with the top picks did not reach their senior seasons: Chris Webber of Michigan, Glenn Robinson of Purdue, and Joe Smith of Maryland. There is no longer the same stigma for those who leave school early as existed twenty years ago, when Indiana Pacers star George McGinnis was referred to as a college "dropout" in the *New York Times*. However, there still is considerable suspicion about whether a high school kid can be ready to play.

Boston Celtics coach M.L. Carr scouted Garnett as a high school player and admired his surprising ballhandling and leaping ability for such a tall player. "The kid's got a lot of skills ... a lot of raw talent," Carr says. The concern Carr had about Garnett's adjustment to the pros was partly about the physical nature of the NBA. "But then there's the off-court situation, which is equally important."

Garnett says he plans to use all his spare time during the season to pursue a college education. "I'm getting my degree. A little piece of paper that says 'Degree' or something. I'm not going to just forget about school." Garnett's multimillion-dollar NBA contract can't buy him a college degree, but it can pay the tuition anywhere he wants to go.

Moses Malone made an effortless transition from high school ball to the NBA.

ABOVE: The sight of Boston Celtics great Larry Bird holding the basketball on the wing, his eyes probing as a teammate cuts toward an open spot, freezes former Cleveland Cavs defender Hot Rod Williams during the 1992 playoffs. OPPOSITE: Chicago Bulls forward Scottie Pippen emerged as a star despite sharing his team with the game's greatest player: Michael Jordan.

touches to his game, making him intriguing enough as a prospect that the Lakers traded for his rights. Nearly unstoppable when he gets the ball near the basket with a defender at his back, Ceballos became an all-star in his first season in LA.

"I have a quiet game. I kind of sneak up on you. I hope there'll be players who try to emulate what I've done, kind of shut-mouth basketball. You don't really try to be flashy and outdo everyone; you want to do whatever you can to get the win and make sure you've left it all on the court. A lot of players want to be flashy. That's okay; I have the ability to do that also, but I choose not to. I conserve my energy and spend it on constantly moving, constantly running. You ask anybody who's played against me, he'll say I'm going to keep moving."

Developing small forward skills is tricky for younger players, because those who wind up at the position at the game's highest levels are usually among the tallest players as they learn the game through grade school and high school. Coaches tend to put the tallest players near the backboard to gather up rebounds. If a player is to become a small forward, he has to work on his own to refine the shooting, passing, and ballhandling skills that are the essential offensive components of the position.

"I played center all through until my junior year," says Dennis Scott of the Orlando Magic, one of the game's greatest shooters. Because he demonstrated such a gift for that part of the game, his coaches allowed him to move away from the basket near the end of his high school career. "I put my time in and practiced, practiced, practiced, and the shooting stroke just came. And here I am today."

The lousy thing about being a small forward is that it means defending against all the other small forwards in the league, a task that can become nearly impossible. "Understand this: no one player is going to stop no one player," said Bernard King, when he was at the height of his high-scoring form in the mid-1980s. "No one player is going to stop me."

King missed two full seasons with injuries, and wasted another because of an alcohol problem, but he still averaged 22.5 points for his career and twice made the All-NBA first team. In good health, King was as dynamic a scorer as any perimeter player in the game's history. He produced points by out-muscling defenders and firing off a speedy succession of jump hooks, a shot that he may not have invented, but that he definitely perfected. His play from the middle of 1984 to the end of 1985 foretold how someone like Michael Jordan could come to dominate the game without having great size in his favor. King averaged 30.1 points in the second half of the 1984 season, 34.8 points in the playoffs—including 42.6 in a playoff victory against Detroit, breaking an NBA record for a five-game series—and 32.9 for 1985.

English of the Denver Nuggets averaged 21.5 points for his career and led the NBA in scoring in 1983, but was always a fine passer and shot blocker. It helps if the player can use his shooting range to draw the defense away from the lane, but a small forward who can dominate the post as Adrian Dantley did during his fifteen NBA seasons can be equally valuable. Dantley was a proficient mid-range jump shooter, but he became one of twenty-one players in the league's history to top 20,000 points primarily because of his knack for using his body and acumen to score inside.

Ceballos has made it with the Lakers by following a similar model. Although he was a productive scorer in college at Cal-State Fullerton, Ceballos wasn't drafted in the NBA's first round because he appeared to lack the shooting range to make it in the league. He was a second-round choice of the Phoenix Suns, which was okay with Ceballos. He scraped his way onto the Suns roster with his hard work in training camp, then listened to what his teammates and coaches taught him. He gradually added small

"It got to the point where he was hitting the shots when he was double- and triple-teamed," said Butch Beard, now the coach of the New Jersey Nets. "It just became an amazing feat to watch an individual get the ball the way he did and be able to get the shot off before the defense could react."

King played the position very differently from most small forwards, who rely on the ability to shoot the ball from the outside and beat their man to the basket, that dual threat causing defenders to be momentarily indecisive and, therefore, doomed. Elgin Baylor of the Los Angeles Lakers was the first of that breed, the first to use his jumping ability to disarm opponents. He was lethal when shooting from the outside, but truly a force in close to the basket. He averaged 13.5 rebounds, despite standing only six feet five inches (195cm), and was selected to the All-NBA first team ten times in the first eleven years of his career. Wilt Chamberlain, Oscar Robertson, Larry Bird, and Magic Johnson cannot say the same.

Connie Hawkins was the next step in the evolution of the small forward, one of the most talented offensive players in the game's history. He could leap and dunk with the highest-flying players in the game's history, but he was tough enough to rebound, and he was an alert, unselfish passer. Many believe Hawkins' flashy style would have enhanced the NBA's popularity a decade earlier than Julius "Dr. J" Erving did, but Hawkins was falsely implicated in a gambling scandal and lost the best years of his career to an unjust ban by the NBA. When he was allowed in the league, Hawkins was no longer the player he'd been because of knee injuries, but he was still good enough to play in four All-Star games. "I've often wondered if he had been able to go through four yeas of college and mature, it would have created one of the all-time great careers," says Phoenix Suns owner Jerry Colangelo.

A lot of Erving's best basketball was lost to history, also, like the great stage performances of such actors as Jason Robards or John Barrymore. Whoever wasn't in the audience that night missed it. Erving played the first five years of his career, when he was young and vital, in the American Basketball Association. He was still a star when the ABA and NBA merged, the league's biggest attraction until Johnson and Bird arrived. Erving was only a serviceable outside shooter, but he was superb on the fast break. He was able to hang in the air and conjure his shots as he flew, grasping the ball in his large hands and always coming up with something to deceive the defense.

When basketball fans talk about Erving, they mostly talk about his style, obscuring the fact that he was one of the game's greatest players. He was a member of two ABA championship teams and one in the NBA, and he led the Philadelphia 76ers to the NBA Finals three times in his eleven seasons. He was twice the ABA's most valuable player, and once in the NBA. In the combined history of the NBA and ABA, only three players have scored more than 30,000 points: Kareem Abdul-Jabbar, Wilt Chamberlain, and Julius Erving.

OPPOSITE: A severe knee injury cut Bernard King's career short and left him just 345 points short of the NBA's exclusive 20,000-point club. ABOVE: Rick Barry was not only Hall of Fame caliber as a player, but as a father: three of his sons became NBA players. TOP: Orlando's Dennis Scott is a long-distance shooting specialist.

Whereas Erving was blessed with style, Rick Barry was cursed with it. He played an artful game; he was a brilliant shooter and passer, and an unyielding worker on the court, but he was equally well known for his temper. The cover of *The Sporting News* once proclaimed him "Mr. Blow-Top." Barry's competitiveness helped to produce a championship for the Golden State Warriors in 1975, when he averaged 30.6 points, 6.2 assists, 5.7 rebounds, and 2.9 steals per game—one of the most amazing seasons ever compiled by a small forward.

It was Barry to whom Bird was most often compared when he entered the NBA, but Bird had the advantage of a calm disposition and a larger physique. Bird, at six feet nine inches (205cm), averaged 10 rebounds per game during his career and blocked a fair number of shots (755) for someone who claimed he couldn't jump. Bird was such an accomplished shooter that he hit nearly 38 percent of his three-point attempts for his career, even though he never got a crack at the more inviting twenty-two-foot (6.7m) line the NBA introduced in 1994. Bird could find openings for passes that few others could conceive. He once jumped to rebound a free throw and fired a pass to a teammate at midcourt without coming back down to the floor.

Upon Bird's departure, it was Grant Hill of the Detroit Pistons who was anointed as the next great small forward. In his rookie season, 1995, he got more votes for the All-Star Game than any veteran. The son of former Dallas Cowboys running back Calvin Hill, Grant is a natural athlete who developed his basketball skills and became such a versatile player that early on he was compared to Michael Jordan.

"It's just too much pressure," Hill contends. "People mean it as a compliment, but one person said it…and now it's like everyone says it. It's not fair to me, and it's not fair to Michael."

The Power Forward

If a basketball coach were to sketch the portrait of the ideal power forward, it would depict a player who stands about six feet nine inches (205cm), weighs 225 pounds (102kg), shoots softly from the corners, and rebounds with ferocity. The picture would look a lot like Maurice Lucas, his face fixed in a menacing scowl.

Lucas, who played his best basketball for the Portland Trail Blazers, averaged 14.6 points and 9.1 rebounds per game for his career and made the All-Star Game five times. He was at least as valuable to his team, and far more renowned, for his ability to intimidate the opposition. Those who dared challenge Lucas or one of his teammates often paid by absorbing a loose forearm or an errant elbow.

When Lucas joined the New York Knicks for the 1981–1982 season, he made a promise to star guard Micheal Ray Richardson. "He told me, 'If there's a guy

ABOVE: Nicknamed "The Enforcer," Maurice Lucas had his superior basketball skills overshadowed by a reputation for muscle and intimidation. OPPOSITE: Vlade Divac of the Lakers struggles to predict what high-flying Seattle SuperSonics forward Shawn Kemp will attempt as he finishes a drive to the basket.

giving you a hard time, just let me know, and I'll set a pick on him and take his head off.'"

He had the attitude and he had the look, but the funny thing about the image of Lucas as the prototype power forward is that there may be no such thing. Of all the positions in basketball, none comes in more shapes and sizes than the power forward. It helps if a power forward is tall, but being shorter than six feet eight inches (203cm) has not handicapped Charles Barkley of the Phoenix Suns or Larry Johnson of the Charlotte Hornets. A wide, muscular frame is common, but Kevin McHale, a seven-time All-Star during his career with the Boston Celtics, was tall and lean, and was more effective for that reason. It's nice to be able to jump for rebounds, but former Celtics great Paul Silas was just as content to clear some space with his strength and let the ball fall into his hands.

Derrick Coleman of the Philadelphia 76ers has all the talents anyone could want in a power forward except, apparently, for a devotion to victory. He has clashed with coaches through most of his pro career, even while produc-

ing 20-point, 11-rebound averages. Shawn Kemp of the Seattle SuperSonics, a six-foot-ten-inch (208cm), 245-pound (111kg) giant, does not have a complete offensive game but runs and jumps like a small forward and scores lots of his points by finishing the fast break. He plays with uncommon enthusiasm. "I'm intense every time I go out there. That's how I play every night."

The one constant with power forwards, though, is that rebounding is job one. Although the center is usually the tallest player on the court, he generally cannot station himself in the best position to grab rebounds because of the defensive demands placed upon him. If the Hornets'

Matt Geiger is busy guarding Houston center Hakeem Olajuwon in the low post, Geiger may be too close to the basket to grab the rebound when Olajuwon shoots. Most misses bounce away from the person who shot the ball, anyway. It's up to Larry Johnson, at six feet seven inches (200cm) and 250 pounds (114kg), to be there to grab it.

"His physical presence and his shoulders, his hips, his legs—that's what strikes you," says Charlotte former Allan Bristow. "If I'm around him, I'm just trying to figure out when I can get to the basketball. And he has tremendous agility. There's no substitute for that degree of quickness…When you combine his athletic ability with a tremendous arm span, well, you just know he'll pull the ball out of the air."

The power forward position began its evolution with Vern Mikkelsen, who played with the Minneapolis Lakers on four NBA championship teams between 1950 and 1954. He was positioned beside six-foot-ten-inch (208cm) center George Mikan, considered the league's first true "big man." Had Mikkelsen played with another team, he might have been a center himself, but his six-foot-seven-inch (200cm), 230-pound (105kg) frame made him perfectly suited for his rebounding specialty.

ABOVE: Charles Barkley of the Phoenix Suns appears too short to be a power forward, but that never seems to be a problem when the games begin and there are rebounds available for him to claim. RIGHT: With his long arms and excellent footwork, Boston Celtics forward Kevin McHale was nearly impossible to stop when he caught the ball in the low post.

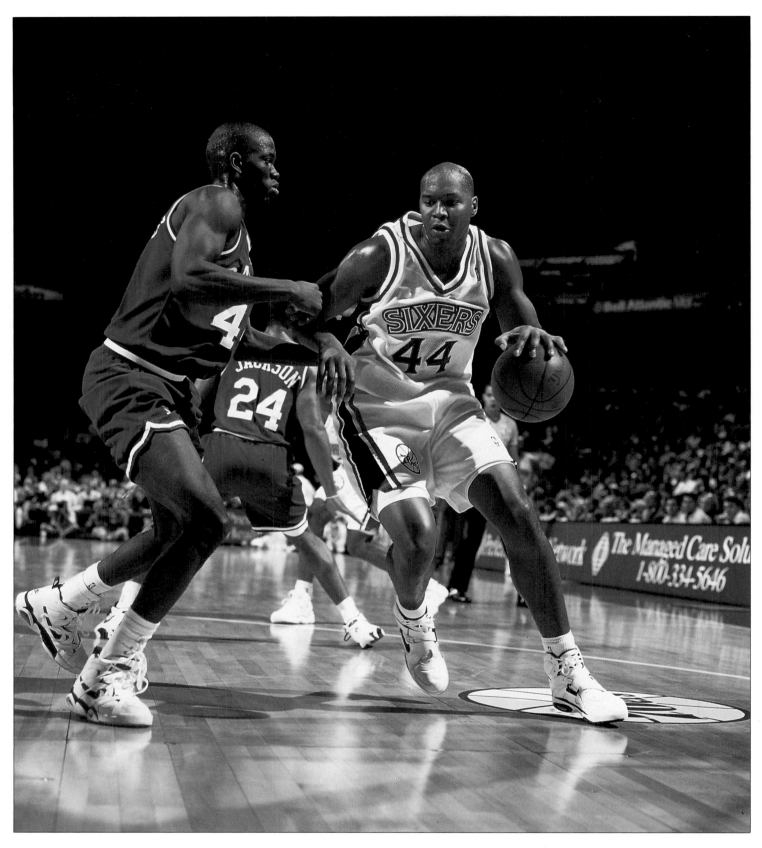

At his best, Philadelphia's Derrick Coleman is one of the most dangerous and versatile power forwards in the NBA.

He wasn't afraid to use his body; he fouled out of more games than any player in the history of the NBA, nearly one time for every 5 games he played.

The position began to mutate when Bob Pettit arrived, demonstrating that a big forward could be much more than just a rebounder (but could still be pretty good at that, too). Pettit, at six feet nine inches (205cm), led the NBA in scoring twice and rebounding once, and is one of six players with more than 20,000 career points and 12,000 rebounds. He was a prelude of sorts to such players as Jerry Lucas of the Cincinnati Royals and New York Knicks, and Elvin Hayes of the Houston Rockets and Washington Bullets. Lucas was among the most versatile power forwards, capable of playing center and equally adept as a shooter, passer, and rebounder. Known as The Big E, Hayes stood six feet ten inches (208cm) and was always more feared by opposing players for his deadly turnaround jumper than for his rebounding, even though

The growth in popularity of weight training gave more players strong-looking bodies after Silas left the game, but Kevin McHale, who became a successor to Silas as the Celtics' power forward, relied more on his long arms and his knowledge of how to score in the low post. McHale stood six feet ten inches (208cm) and tormented smaller forwards with his shot-blocking ability on defense and his knack for scoring inside.

The antithesis of McHale, at least physically, is Karl Malone. Despite the fact that Malone stands six feet nine inches (205cm), weighs 255 pounds (116kg), and had a superb college career at Louisiana Tech, twelve teams passed him up in the 1985 draft, leaving him as a gift to the Utah Jazz. His hard-driving style and imposing physique—and the benefit of playing with point guard John Stockton—has made Malone one of the best offensive power forwards ever to play.

Charles Barkley could play either forward position, but his love for rebounding nudged him toward the power spot. He is not quite six feet five inches (195cm) tall, but he led the NBA in rebounding in his third season. He is among the most versatile offensive players in the league, capable of scoring from the low post, on three-point shots, or by backing down his man with the dribble and firing a fadeaway jump shot. For all his basketball skill and accomplishments, Barkley's unique personality has earned him at least as much attention. He is gifted and cursed with a drive to say what he thinks, which endears him to some fans and alienates him from others. In the 1992 Olympics, he was criticized for elbowing a player from Angola, which drew a technical foul. "Somebody hits me, I'm going to hit them back," Barkley says.

Maurice Lucas, who retired in 1988, always believed in being a silent force. He was more likely to warn an opponent with a frightening look than with a loud threat. His style made him as quietly effective as any power forward in basketball. "If I see a guy who's not as strong as I am, I'm going to take advantage of that," Lucas said when he played. "This game is all about taking advantage of what you get and what the opponents give you." However, he does not mind being remembered for his attitude.

"I just hope fans remember me. This is a funny business, and people remember you for a couple of years, and only the true basketball fans will remember you after that. They can remember me for whatever they want."

ABOVE: Dave DeBusschere drove his way to seven All-Star games and two championship rings in an eleven-year career with the Pistons and Knicks. OPPOSITE: The sight of Utah's Karl Malone driving through the lane on a fastbreak can cause even Shaquille O'Neal to clear a path for "The Mailman."

only three players in the history of the league, centers Wilt Chamberlain, Bill Russell, and Kareem Abdul-Jabbar, collected more rebounds.

The New York Knicks' Dave DeBusschere was kind of a shrunken-down version of Shawn Kemp, standing six feet six inches (198cm) but capable of running opponents to exhaustion in the late 1960s and early 1970s. He was a fine scorer and passer, like most of his peers, who gained recognition as a power forward. Paul Silas of the Boston Celtics, however, was the first to be fairly average as a shooter and passer but to prove his value as an expert rebounder. Only once in his career did Silas average 15 points per game, but he routinely was among the top boardmen in the NBA. Silas understood the science of rebounding; he pointed out that most rebounds were taken below the rim, so it mattered more which player was in position to grab the ball than which could jump up to catch it: "How you use your body is very important."

Despite doubters who believed he could only play power forward in the NBA, Alonzo Mourning left Georgetown prepared to be a pro center.

The Center

The smile belongs to a child: wild, innocent, boundlessly joyful. The rest of Shaquille O'Neal is all man, and has been since he was a teenager, since he stood on the court to practice for the Dapper Dan high school all-star game in Pittsburgh and so clearly stood out from players who were ostensibly his peers.

He stood seven feet one inch (215cm) even then, but has only grown larger over time, from 270 pounds (123kg) of lean muscle as a senior at Cole High in San Antonio to three hundred pounds (136kg) of unbridled power as a young veteran with the Orlando Magic. O'Neal can be offered as the perfect evidence that being tall isn't enough to become a great basketball center, because there are lots of seven-footers (213cm) hanging around the game, but there's only one Shaq.

O'Neal was largely responsible for the resurgence in the importance of a great center in the game of basketball after nearly a decade in which the position's impact had dwindled. Larry Bird, Magic Johnson, and Michael Jordan had turned the focus of the game toward the versa-

tile perimeter player. The Chicago Bulls won three consecutive NBA Finals from 1991 to 1993 with aging veteran Bill Cartwright as their primary center. He didn't average as much as 10 points per game in any of those seasons. The Detroit Pistons won the two titles before that with Bill Laimbeer, who was tough around the basket but scored most of his 12 points per game on twenty-foot (6.1m) jump shots.

As this developed, it also became fashionable for players who grew to be seven feet (213cm) tall or close to it to disdain the idea of playing center. A proficient center will work hard to establish position in the low post, his

Phoenix forward Charles Barkley considers whether to challenge Orlando center Shaquille O'Neal, whose 300-pound (136kg) presence discourages most opponents from attacking the Magic on the inside.

back to the basket, then quickly or forcefully launch a clear shot or fire a pass to a teammate open on the perimeter or cutting toward the goal. Playing center requires nearly as much knowledge of the game as is demanded of the point guard. It was for all these reasons that a generation of big men worked on their jumpshots so they could play power forward, and avoided mastering post moves so that their coaches would keep them out of the middle.

"Big men today don't know how to play big," says Mel Daniels, who played with the Indiana Pacers and ranks as the greatest center in ABA history. "They want to go outside and shoot jump shots, handle the ball like guards. They don't play with the same force and enthusiasm. They're so big in high school, they get away with a lot of things they shouldn't be doing. When I was in high school, my job was to rebound, block shots, score when I had to. If you were a big guy, you stayed your butt in the paint."

Lorenzen Wright, who stands six feet eleven inches (210cm), began his progress toward an NBA career as a center at the University of Memphis. He believes fear

By sealing off Glen Whisby of Southern Mississippi, center Lorenzen Wright of Memphis establishes the sort of low-post position that can force an opposing defense to break down.

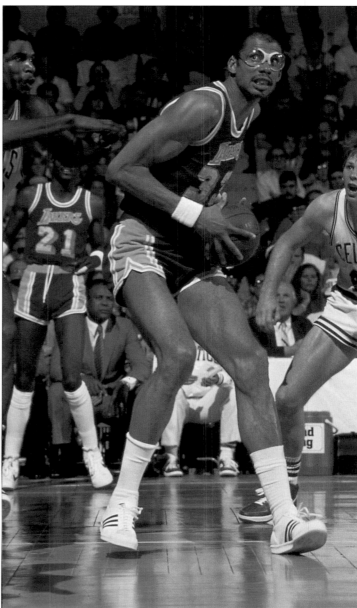

Through the late 1970s and early 1980s, the Lakers' Kareem Abdul-Jabbar reigned as the one enduring, dominant center in the NBA.

keeps many players his size away from the lane. "I think the people who don't want to be centers are the people who are scared to be centers. They see the big guys out there banging, and I think they chicken out."

It was curious that this phenomenon developed in direct correlation to the fortunes of seven-foot-two-inch (218cm) Kareem Abdul-Jabbar, who dominated the center position through the 1970s with his precision, coordination, and technique. He played at a time when the position was manned by the likes of six-foot-eleven-inch (210cm) Bob Lanier, a massive left-hander who used his soft shooting touch to play his way into the Hall of Fame; six-foot-nine-inch (205cm) Dave Cowens, a Hall of Famer who specialized in running the opposing center into exhaustion; and Wes Unseld, an amazing passer and rebounder and, at six feet seven inches (200cm), perhaps the smallest great center in the game's history. Bill Walton

OPPOSITE: He led the NBA in field goal shooting in 1994, but Orlando center Shaquille O'Neal is often criticized for being able to do little more than dunk.

played the position as well as anyone could from 1975 through 1978, but his career was spoiled by injuries. Abdul-Jabbar was the preeminent player of the time. He developed the sky hook, perhaps the most devastating offensive weapon in the game's history, responsible for so many of his career-record 38,387 points. Abdul-Jabbar was named the NBA's Most Valuable Player six times, was a member of six NBA champions and three NCAA champions, and was inducted into the Hall of Fame in 1995.

By the time he was finishing his career with the Lakers, however, Abdul-Jabbar had long ceased to be the dominant player on his team. It was Magic Johnson's show. Abdul-Jabbar was still a productive offensive player until his final year, but the Lakers had changed and so, too, had basketball. From 1979 through 1989, Moses Malone and Hakeem Olajuwon were the only dominant centers in the league. Malone, with the Houston Rockets and then the Philadelphia 76ers, was the very picture of the immovable low-post object, never a smooth offensive player but so forceful that he could not be denied the nearly 30,000 points he accumulated. "He was just so tough to box out because he was so quick," says Tree Rollins, a seven-foot-one-inch (215cm) center who lasted nearly two decades in the NBA. "He was real physical, one of the toughest guys for me to deal with."

Olajuwon joined the Rockets soon after Malone departed in 1982, displacing seven-foot-four-inch (223cm) Ralph Sampson and developing into one of the greatest centers in the game's history. Those two were about it for the longest time. Scouts still looked for big players whenever possible, bringing fine players like Brad Daugherty of the Cleveland Cavaliers, Patrick Ewing of the New York Knicks, and Robert Parish of the Boston Celtics into the league, but the teams winning championships were doing it from the perimeter.

O'Neal's arrival in the NBA showed teams how the future would look, that it would be a good deal more like the past. He was only twenty years old when he played his first game with the Orlando Magic, scoring 12 points and getting 18 rebounds in a 110–100 win over Miami on No-

vember 6, 1992. If the other teams in the league were going to contend with Orlando, they would surely have to deal with O'Neal. He is the most astonishing specimen of strength, grace, and agility to arrive in basketball since Wilt Chamberlain four decades earlier, and as such has faced much of the same hostility.

It is not that people dislike O'Neal. He is considered reasonably genial, at times ebullient. It's just that whatever he does, it can never be enough. To look at him is to be certain he ought to be capable of doing more. When O'Neal undertakes any project outside of basketball, from acting in the motion picture *Blue Chips* to cutting a rap record, *Shaq Diesel*, detractors claim that time should be spent on improving as a basketball player, especially as a foul shooter. His coach at Louisiana State, Dale Brown, predicted when O'Neal turned professional, "A wonderful performance isn't enough. There will be demands for superhuman performances."

The same was expected of Chamberlain throughout his career, but then, he so often delivered. Chamberlain is

Hakeem Olajuwon grew quickly into the center position after arriving in the U.S. from Nigeria, making three trips to the NCAA Final Four with the University of Houston.

San Antonio's David Robinson, wrestling the New York Knicks' Anthony Mason, plays center like an oversized small forward—which he is.

uncommon grace and quickness for someone his size. It was then that he more or less invented the finger-roll shot, which involved standing in the lane and leaning toward the basket with his arm extended and the ball sitting in his palm, then cocking the wrist so the ball rolled down his fingers and into the net. Chamberlain went on to attend Kansas University, scored 52 points in his first game, and averaged 29.9 points per game in the two seasons he played before choosing to leave school early and play with the Harlem Globetrotters.

George Mikan and Bob Kurland were considered the first great big men in basketball; the six-foot-ten-inch (208cm) Mikan established a more prominent place in history by playing in the NBA and leading the Minneapolis Lakers to five championships, whereas Kurland went into business and played for a company team. Chamberlain, though, was the first great basketball player who was a big man. He is the only player ever to lead the NBA in scoring, rebounding, and assists for at least one season, and still is the only center to lead in assists. He led the league in scoring seven times and rebounding eleven times. Tom Gola, a Hall of Famer himself, called Chamberlain "the greatest basketball player that ever lived."

the only man to score 100 points in a professional game. He produced the four highest single-season scoring averages in the NBA's history, including a numbing 50.4 points in 1961–1962. The year before, he averaged a record 27.2 rebounds. Five times in the past dozen years, the NBA rebounding champion did not pull in half that many.

Chamberlain was born in Philadelphia and attended Overbrook High, where he first established his dominance as a basketball player. He wasn't the tower of strength he would become as a professional, but Chamberlain already had huge hands and

Anyone looking for a good argument on the subject, however, should be able to find a few people who will contend Chamberlain wasn't even the best of his time. Bill Russell didn't score half as many points as Chamberlain, but he had this amazing habit of winning championships wherever he played. At the University of San Francisco, he was the center on two NCAA champions, his team winning 55 consecutive games between 1954 and 1956. Russell played for the United States in the 1956 Olympics at Melbourne, Australia, earning a gold medal. His legacy only grew when he arrived in the pros. Russell was the focus of eleven NBA champion Celtic teams, serving as player-coach for two of those teams (1968 and 1969).

Russell was never the same offensive force as Chamberlain, but he didn't try to be and didn't need to be. Instead, Russell was the first dominant defensive player, controlling the lane with his ability to block shots and squeeze opposing centers out of position. Whereas today's centers often reject shots for intimidation or for show, Russell was alert enough to tip his blocks toward teammates so they could start fast breaks. Russell also understood that rebounding is one of the key elements of an effective defense, averaging 22.5 per game during his thirteen-year career. He made the NBA's all-defensive team only once, but that was because no one had the vision to invent such an honor until Russell's final season, 1969.

Russell became the progenitor of a legion of big men whose bodies grew more quickly than their basketball skills. When Patrick Ewing left Rindge & Latin High School in Cambridge, Massachusetts, in 1981, he was relatively new to the game, but was so clearly an overwhelming talent that Georgetown University, a school with great academic prestige, agreed to special conditions for his education established by his high school advisors. Ewing arrived at Georgetown as a spectacular shot blocker, but not an imposing offensive player. He averaged only 12.7 points in his first season (and never more than 17.7 in college) but was such a force on defense that the Hoyas made three Final Four trips during his career and won the 1984 NCAA Championship.

In the NBA, Ewing developed a consistent eighteen-foot (5.5m) jumper and, as his legs gradually weakened, became better known for his ability on offense than on defense. "He's a hard worker. He's a winner. He's a physical player," said Hakeem Olajuwon, who faced Ewing in the 1984 NCAA title game and the 1994 NBA Finals. "He's tough mentally and just a tough competitor."

Ewing was followed at Georgetown by two other players in the Russell mold, Alonzo Mourning and Dikembe Mutombo. In his four years of college, Mourning became the NCAA's career leader in blocked shots. Mutombo, who was born in Zaire, had a limited basketball background when he was found by Georgetown coach John Thompson, but quickly grasped the technique of properly blocking shots. He grew from there into a superior defender with the Denver Nuggets of the NBA, leading the league in blocks in his third pro season and averaging more than a dozen rebounds per game.

The ranks of basketball big men are full of players with unusual stories like Mutombo's. Manute Bol, at seven feet seven inches (231cm) the tallest player ever to compete in the NBA, who was born in the Sudan and was largely unfamiliar with basketball, was discovered by a touring coach, who helped arrange to have him come to the United States to play the sport in college. Bol played one season at the University of Bridgeport, then entered the NBA draft and became the league leader in blocked shots for two seasons, 1986 and 1989.

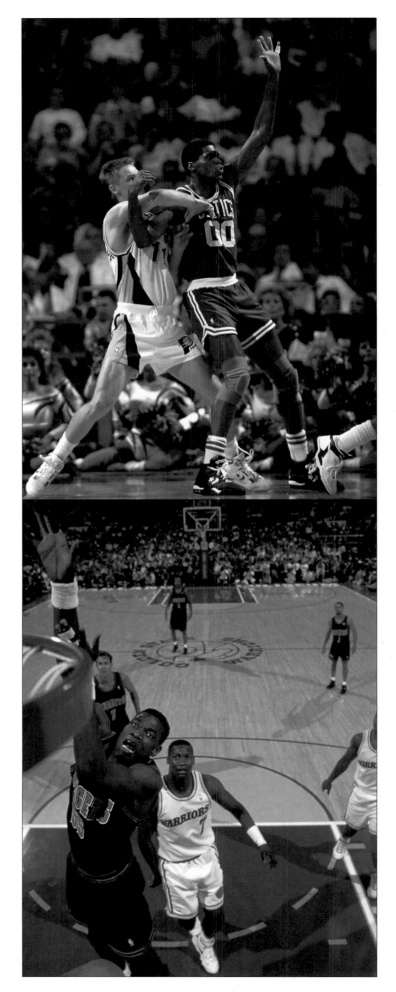

As an agile, athletic seven-footer (213cm), center Wilt Chamberlain (opposite) was so far ahead of his time, he once averaged 50 points a game through an entire NBA season. Whether it is Rik Smits of the Indiana Pacers wrestling with veteran Robert Parish over low-post position (top) or Dikembe Mutombo of the Denver Nuggets launching a twisting jump-hook from just beneath the goal (above), the seven-foot center has become a regular part of the NBA landscape. However, size does not guarantee success in the league, which also demands superior skills, intensity, and an understanding of how to play the inside game.

Houston star Hakeem Olajuwon, a deft shooter and ballhandler, is one center who never has been rooted to the low post.

Hakeem Olajuwon arrived at the University of Houston with unquestioned athletic skills: he had played soccer for years as a goalie. He had played little basketball, however, and was so raw that he barely played during his first two years in college. In his final two years, he was among the best players in the country, and became the first player chosen in the NBA draft—ahead of Michael Jordan. Olajuwon was quicker than some of his contemporaries to grasp the basics of offensive basketball. He left college with a dynamic turnaround jump shot and with excellent shooting range.

Olajuwon is listed at seven feet (213cm), but most consider him to be no taller than six feet ten inches (208cm). It hasn't mattered. Olajuwon is the foremost center of his era, never averaging fewer than 20 points nor fewer than 10 rebounds per game. "Hakeem's awesome," says Orlando Magic guard Anfernee Hardaway. "The things he does, you don't have to classify him as a center." Olajuwon was the most valuable player during the playoffs as Houston won the NBA title in 1994 and 1995. "He can do it all—left side, right side. He can dribble. He has a complete game," says O'Neal, who saw Olajuwon make moves he's never seen from another player. "Hakeem is a great player, the best."

Although David Robinson played a lot of basketball before he arrived at the Naval Academy, he never figured he'd wind up as an all-star center in the NBA. He stood only six feet seven inches (200cm) as a high school senior. Paul Evans, the coach who recruited him to Navy, said he hoped Robinson would be an athletic small forward when he made the decision to sign him. Robinson grew to six feet ten inches (208cm) by the end of his freshman year, eventually settling at seven feet one inch (215cm). And he kept all of the quickness and running, jumping, and shooting ability that made him attractive as a perimeter player.

As O'Neal entered the league, it was Robinson, Olajuwon, and Ewing that he was measured against, and he

quickly proved to be their equal. In his third season, 1995, he led the NBA in scoring and led Orlando to the NBA Finals—long before reaching his potential as a player. "Shaquille doesn't really know the game of basketball," says Tree Rollins, an Orlando assistant coach. "Penny Hardaway is always studying the game, but everything with the big fella is so God-given. On offense, he's always focused on where the ball is. If we can get him to do that on defense, we'll have what everyone wants, a complete basketball player."

Off the court, O'Neal has become the biggest star since Michael Jordan, endorsing sneakers, fast food, and two different beverages. Although he is eager to accept commercial endorsements that are offered to him, O'Neal claims no desire to replace Jordan as the NBA's reigning superstar or even Chamberlain as basketball's historic Goliath. "I'm not looking to do that," O'Neal says. "I'm just trying to go out and take care of my own business."

Patrick Ewing's ability to frighten Georgetown opponents with his defensive intensity and offensive power made him one of the premier college players of the 1980s.

CHAPTER FIVE

The Coach

H is last team in Cleveland won 54 games, fifth-best among teams in the NBA in the 1992–1993 season, leaving Lenny Wilkens within a couple of decent seasons of setting the career record for victories by a professional coach. So he did what any winning coach would do in those circumstances. He resigned.

The Cleveland Cavaliers were nowhere when Wilkens became their coach in 1986, but he turned them into a machine that won 50 games or more three times and reached the Eastern Conference finals in 1992. What neither he nor any other human could do was lift the Cavs past Michael Jordan and the Chicago Bulls; Jordan knocked out Cleveland four times in five seasons, including a 4–0 sweep in Wilkens' final year. The Cleveland organization decided it would need some other coach's approach if the Cavaliers were ever to overtake Chicago. Wilkens then said he "thought it best" to resign.

Upon moving to a position as head coach of the Atlanta Hawks, Wilkens drove the mediocre team to 57 victories and was named the NBA's coach of the year. Midway through his second season, Wilkens passed Red Auerbach of the Boston Celtics to set the career wins record with 939. "As well as I love Red," Wilkens said afterward, "he never had to coach as many bad teams as I have."

This is the coach's curse: however many games he wins, the fans and the boss will figure he loses a lot more. Pat Riley, the handsome and successful coach of four NBA championship teams with the Los Angeles Lakers, once said, "There are two things in coaching: there is winning and there is misery." The players who shoot and rebound the basketball get the credit for victories, which is as it should be, but the coach's name is the one mentioned when things don't go as well.

Coaches at the college and professional levels are well-paid for their troubles, and that is not the only compensation. There is the respect of peers and superiors. There is the satisfaction of working with gifted ath-

Coaching styles in the NBA range from the cool, corporate image presented by Pat Riley of the Miami Heat (left) to the inspirational fire of former Philadelphia 76ers coach John Lucas (above), who was as active on the sideline as players are on the court. But what never changes is that no one approach offers the universal key to victory.

letes; the best of coaches not only make teams better, they make players better, which is one of Wilkens' most valuable skills. And there is victory, a reward in itself.

A coach can be a screamer like the University of Cincinnati's Bob Huggins or as quiet as the great John Wooden of UCLA. He can order a tightly orchestrated style of play, like the New York Knicks' Hall of Famer Red Holzman, or a free-form, run-and-gun game like former Denver Nuggets coach Doug Moe. Players believe in University of Indiana's Bob Knight because they respect his knowledge; they believe in Philadelphia 76ers coach John Lucas because he so obviously respects them.

There is no one recipe for greatness, but so many of the ingredients are the same: dedication, vision, communication, and a fanatical devotion to the game. You will find these qualities in most successful coaches. To those who take the trouble to notice any of them, the coaches are most grateful.

The Geniuses

Basketball fans keep trying to figure out why Larry Brown rarely coaches in the same place for more than a few years at a time. He never gives a good answer, but it shouldn't be that hard to figure out. Genius is like that. A genius not only knows things others wouldn't conceive, he often does things others wouldn't consider. Like moving eight times in twenty-one years, covering the United States from New York to Los Angeles, with North Carolina, Indiana, Kansas, and Colorado in between.

Wherever Brown lands, he emerges as a winner. Genius, in basketball, is like that, too. He drove two different teams in the American Basketball Association to first place, led the University of Kansas to the 1988 NCAA title, and won better than 500 games and earned five first-place finishes in eleven NBA seasons. He even made the Los Angeles Clippers a winning team, which is proof enough of his brilliance. There isn't a particular Larry Brown style; he is a master of assessing the available talent and drawing from each player that which can make the team function most efficiently. Brown's championship Kansas team featured one dominant player, All-American forward Danny Manning, a capable point guard in Kevin Pritchard, and a half-dozen others who might not have been good enough to play for teams that weren't good enough to reach the tournament. "He gets everybody to play together," says Vern Fleming, a guard for Brown's successful Indiana Pacers teams.

"I don't think there's a coach in the United States better than Larry," says Donnie Walsh, the Pacers president and Brown's longtime friend. "Larry sees the game very fundamentally. He has a tremendous amount of knowledge that he's able to give to players in a very concrete simplistic way. A true genius can make things that are complex seem simple."

Larry Brown (top) and Mike Krzyzewski (above) both have coached teams to NCAA championships, but whereas Brown is at least as well known for how frequently he changes jobs, Krzyzewski has turned down numerous offers to move and has remained in place at Duke University. OPPOSITE: Arkansas coach Nolan Richardson has a way of getting his players to believe the players on the other team hate them, then convincing them to unleash that anger on those unfortunate opponents.

Former Marquette coach Al McGuire left the game exactly as any coach would want to leave: he led his team to the 1977 NCAA championship and a convincing victory over North Carolina.

The components of a successful coach are difficult to recognize because coaches arrive at victory by so many different avenues. The genius separates himself by always managing to stay ahead of the opposition and the game, and by frequently neglecting other necessities of life. Mike Krzyzewski, who led Duke University to seven Final Fours and two NCAA championships in nine seasons, was in such a rush to return to work after back surgery in 1995 that he ignored the doctor's recommendation to wait two months, and was back on the job in two weeks. Overcome by exhaustion, he was forced to leave the team at midseason.

Another clue, though, is that restlessness. University of Arkansas coach Nolan Richardson is the only person to win the championships of the national junior college tournament, the National Invitation Tournament, and the NCAA. He instituted an unpredictable full-court press he calls "Forty Minutes of Hell," and proved that winning teams needn't run a structured offense nor rebound especially well. He frequently threatens to leave coaching, though, or to leave Arkansas for another job.

That inability to stay in place has caused some of coaching's most brilliant minds to leave the game before it might have been necessary. Al McGuire won 79 percent of

his games in thirteen seasons at Marquette University, including the 1977 NCAA championship in his final season, but retired before he reached his forty-ninth birthday. He became a businessman and television commentator. The most accomplished of all NBA coaches, Red Auerbach of the Boston Celtics, put together the greatest dynasty in the history of team sports and won nine championships in ten years between 1957 and 1966, but left coaching to run the Celtics from the front office at the exact same age as McGuire.

Auerbach was voted the greatest coach in NBA history by the Pro Basketball Writers' Association in 1980. He invented the concept of the "sixth man," holding a top

Former Marquette coach Al McGuire left the game exactly as any coach would want to leave: he led his team to the 1977 NCAA championship and a convincing victory over North Carolina.

The components of a successful coach are difficult to recognize because coaches arrive at victory by so many different avenues. The genius separates himself by always managing to stay ahead of the opposition and the game, and by frequently neglecting other necessities of life. Mike Krzyzewski, who led Duke University to seven Final Fours and two NCAA championships in nine seasons, was in such a rush to return to work after back surgery in 1995 that he ignored the doctor's recommendation to wait two months, and was back on the job in two weeks. Overcome by exhaustion, he was forced to leave the team at midseason.

Another clue, though, is that restlessness. University of Arkansas coach Nolan Richardson is the only person to win the championships of the national junior college tournament, the National Invitation Tournament, and the NCAA. He instituted an unpredictable full-court press he calls "Forty Minutes of Hell," and proved that winning teams needn't run a structured offense nor rebound especially well. He frequently threatens to leave coaching, though, or to leave Arkansas for another job.

That inability to stay in place has caused some of coaching's most brilliant minds to leave the game before it might have been necessary. Al McGuire won 79 percent of

his games in thirteen seasons at Marquette University, including the 1977 NCAA championship in his final season, but retired before he reached his forty-ninth birthday. He became a businessman and television commentator. The most accomplished of all NBA coaches, Red Auerbach of the Boston Celtics, put together the greatest dynasty in the history of team sports and won nine championships in ten years between 1957 and 1966, but left coaching to run the Celtics from the front office at the exact same age as McGuire.

Auerbach was voted the greatest coach in NBA history by the Pro Basketball Writers' Association in 1980. He invented the concept of the "sixth man," holding a top

No basketball coach was better at teaching his players defense than Henry Iba, who guided Oklahoma A&M (now Oklahoma State) to two NCAA titles and four Final Four appearances.

player from the starting lineup for an immediate infusion of energy as the other team tired. He first presented the "post-up" concept, moving the center away from the goal to allow a strong guard to take his defensive man inside and muscle home a score. He was always searching for an edge, which is why the visiting locker room at the old Boston Garden was about the size of a bathroom stall and was always either too hot or too cold, depending on the weather. For all he knew about the game, though, Auerbach listened to his players' suggestions in huddles and respected their ideas.

When Auerbach had had enough of coaching, he turned to running the team, and was responsible for trades that brought stars like Robert Parish, Kevin McHale, and Dennis Johnson to the Celtics in return for little of value. When other teams were concerned with obstacles that might have kept Larry Bird and Danny Ainge from providing immediate help, Auerbach boldly drafted both players and made them part of the Celtics organization. In the 1980s, the Celtics added three more championship banners to their collection of sixteen on the ceiling of the Garden.

When John Wooden was coach at UCLA, he stressed team play above all else despite coaching some of the most gifted players in history: Kareem Abdul-Jabbar, Gail Goodrich, Bill Walton, and Walt Hazzard.

Phog Allen of Kansas, Hank Iba of Oklahoma State, and Adolph Rupp were the first generation of coaching geniuses. Pete Newell carried on that tradition as he coached and continued to give advice during his retirement. He was among the first to stress full-court zone pressure in college basketball, that tactic becoming a key to his University of California team winning the 1960 NCAA championship. He did not stay on the job long, though, winning 234 games in fourteen seasons at San Francisco, Michigan State, and California. Three decades after his retirement, Newell's coaching mind remains a valuable resource for his disciples. And his theories on center play have brought some of the most talented big

men in the game—including NBA all-star Shaquille O'Neal—to his annual summer teaching camp.

Not all of coaching's geniuses are so mobile. Jack Ramsay lasted eleven seasons at St. Joseph's and put together a 234–72 record before moving to the NBA, where he earned 864 wins in twenty-one seasons. He blended the 1977 Portland Trail Blazers into one of the NBA's consummate teams, each player devoted to his role and to the common goal. Among college coaches, John Wooden lasted at UCLA from 1948 through 1975. North Carolina's Dean Smith continued past his sixty-fifth birthday. Bob Knight, the volatile coach at Indiana, has been there for more than two decades, perhaps partly as a stubborn rejection of those in the media who have called on him to leave his post.

Wooden, looking aged and fragile well into his eighties, still sits behind the UCLA bench at Pauley Pavilion as the Bruins play each winter. But then, that was how John Wooden looked when he was on the UCLA bench compiling the greatest record of any college basketball coach. He won ten NCAA championships while seated in his chair with his legs tightly crossed and a game program gripped in his hand, always wearing a calm expression. He has never allowed himself to venture far from the game in the two decades since his retirement, and the game hasn't wandered far from where he left it.

The imprint of Wooden's brilliance has been left on most of the college basketball champions since he stopped coaching, even those teams whose coaches weren't students or close friends of Wooden. He was a coach who made the full-court press a primary defensive weapon, but he never believed in the idea of coaching genius. He instead stressed conditioning, attention to offensive and defensive fundamentals, and appreciation of the team concept. He drilled those elements into his players with grueling, intense practices. Wooden was so particular about details, he even instructed players regarding how to properly wear their socks.

It definitely didn't hurt that he had Lew Alcindor (now Kareem Abdul-Jabbar) and Bill Walton, two of the greatest college centers, to help win five of the Bruins' NCAA titles, but they also won two with six-foot-five-inch (195cm) Keith Erickson in the middle and two more with six-foot-nine-inch (205cm) Steve Patterson, who was never an All-American.

Wooden's achievements have haunted the coaches who succeeded him, even though some were largely responsible for his success. Gary Cunningham was one of Wooden's top assistants. Larry Farmer and Walt Hazzard were star players. The pressure of trying to recapture Wooden's legend undid them. Jim Harrick has been a friend of Wooden's for years, but he struggled to survive criticism even while attempting to embrace Wooden's legacy.

"He does not give advice concerning basketball matters," says Harrick, whose team won the NCAA title in 1995. "He gives opinions, but not advice. Probably 95 percent of the things we do offensively, I call the John Wooden system. The fundamentals, conditioning, team play—and certainly his drills. We use them all. He perfected them. The system is really sound and solid. I like having him come and enjoy our games, because he's meant a lot to me, to the university, and certainly to basketball."

Dean Smith's success as a college coach at North Carolina has been so steady that he was elected to the Hall of Fame just before winning the first of his two NCAA titles. He has been among the most innovative college coaches, using a defensive system that emphasizes trapping the player with the ball and forcing unwise decisions, and an offense that requires near-constant motion and alert passing. In the mid-seventies, Smith perfected the "four-corners" delay offense, placing point guard Phil Ford at the center of the court and requesting him to dribble away several minutes at a time, until he was fouled or penetrated to the goal for a layup. It was the perfect device for protecting a lead, until the colleges decided to institute a shot clock to eliminate such stalling.

Smith is not unlike Wooden in his ability to drive his theories of basketball into the minds of his players, but Smith has been more rigid about the type of offense his team plays and has favored half-court pressure defense to keep the game's pace more under control. Smith and North Carolina won the NCAA title in 1982 and 1993 and made the Final Four ten times. For thirteen consecutive seasons, between 1981 and 1993, the Tar Heels made it to the NCAA Tournament's second round of sixteen teams.

"He made us a great team," says Matt Doherty, a power forward for the 1982 champions. "The things he instilled in us— the unselfishness and the competitiveness—made us a great team. It was just everyday reminders in practice, the constant talk about moving the basketball, getting a good shot."

Smith has been so successful attracting talented players to Chapel

Adolph Rupp ruled Kentucky basketball in such an autocratic fashion he came to be known as "the Baron." He established UK as the one school in the Southeastern Conference where basketball, not football, was clearly the preeminent sport.

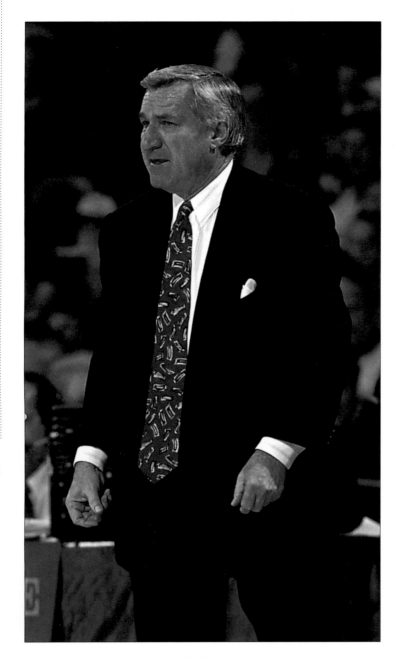

North Carolina's Dean Smith consistently molds his players into a cohesive unit.

Hill, however, that it's not hard to find basketball fans who believe the Tar Heels should have won more. Michael Jordan played three seasons there, but only made the Final Four once. Brad Daugherty, who became an all-star center in the NBA, never made it. When Jordan got to the pros, the joke began that the only person on the planet capable of holding him under 20 points was Dean Smith. The criticism was aimed less at Smith than at his "system," and it bothered him so much that he insisted there was no "system."

Even players who lasted only a season at North Carolina will say Smith has a specific way he demands things be done. "At Carolina, they may have one great athlete, but all five players are going to come at you as one machine," says Cliff Rozier, a forward for the Golden State Warriors. He played one season for Smith before transferring to Louisville. "It takes everybody to be on the same page for that machine to work."

Smith's players have defended him as being "like a father figure," which is how All-American forward Jerry Stackhouse put it. "He teaches us a lot, not only about

basketball, but about other things…He scolds us, but he picks us up when we're down." Rasheed Wallace, Stackhouse's teammate on the 1995 Final Four team, called Smith "a phenomenal coach."

Most of those outside the Indiana program have been unable to determine why players keep joining the Hoosiers and subjecting themselves to the verbal assaults from Knight that are a regular feature of practices and games. Knight is the ultimate perfectionist, always searching for his players to achieve a flawless performance, always frustrated by their inability to attain that goal in

He can be charming or crass, pleasant or profane, but there is nothing ambiguous about Bob Knight's coaching ability. His Indiana Hoosiers have dominated the Big Ten Conference for the better part of two decades and won three NCAA championships.

spite of three NCAA Championships. His teams invariably play man-to-man defense; on offense, they run teams through a maze of screens to free the Hoosiers for open jumpshots. It can be maddening to play against Knight's teams and maddening to play for him, but those who survive in the program believe strongly in his message.

"You've never heard one negative thing from a guy who's played for Coach Knight for four years," says Joby Wright, who played for Knight, coached with him as an assistant, and went on to become coach at the University of Wyoming. "Coach is really misunderstood for a lot of reasons, but I think if you could talk to a player who played for him for four years, you'll hear, 'Yeah, we had some times that were tough and times when I didn't understand what was going on, but I appreciated learning that everything that is worthwhile has a price.'"

Born Winners

Chuck Daly was still in ninth grade when he realized what he wanted to do with the rest of his life. "I told my mother, 'I want to be a college coach and make ten thousand dollars a year.'" He shot a little low on both counts.

After starting his career at Punxsutawney High School in northwest Pennsylvania, Daly did become a college coach, spending eight seasons at the University of Pennsylvania and compiling a 151–62 record. He led the Quakers to the NCAA Tournament in four consecutive seasons (1972–1975) and nearly made the Final Four in his first tournament appearance.

A major college job places a coach among the elite, but that's not as exclusive a club as coaching in the National Basketball Association, which is where Daly wound up achieving his greatest results and making a lot more than ten grand. He left Penn to become a pro assistant and eventually took over as coach of the Detroit Pistons, where he won two NBA titles and earned the opportunity to be selected as coach of the 1992 U.S. Olympic team, the Dream Team, considered to be the greatest collection of talent in the game's history.

Daly didn't have to do much with that group. "You'll see other teams of professionals, but you won't see a team quite like this," he said in Barcelona, after the Dream Team clinched the gold medal. With Detroit, however, Daly conceived the bruising defensive style that made the Pistons the NBA's Bad Boys. He proved his coaching skill for certain when he left the Pistons and became coach of the New Jersey Nets. His unusual ability to communicate with young players led to the Nets posting consecutive winning seasons and playoff appearances in his two years there, after seven straight years of sub-.500 ball.

Chuck Daly coached the Detroit Pistons' "Bad Boys" and the original U.S. Olympic Dream Team, and in both cases epitomized the modern coach who could comfortably communicate with young players and seasoned veterans.

Pat Riley's impact has been immediate each time he has taken over a new team: in Los Angeles, New York, and Miami.

Some coaches have that ability, to carry victory with them wherever they go. They may not have a distinctive style or a lasting impact on the style of basketball that is played by others. They might have borrowed the basics of their approaches from other coaches they admire. But they always win.

After claiming four NBA titles with the Los Angeles Lakers, Pat Riley became coach of the New York Knicks in 1991 and turned them from a team that finished 14 games under .500 (39–43) to one that was 20 games better than .500 (51–31). Lenny Wilkens took over the Seattle SuperSonics in 1977, when they held a 5–17 record. They were 42–18 in their next 60 games.

Dick Motta has coached the Chicago Bulls, the Washington Bullets, and the Dallas Mavericks in two separate stints and won more games than all but two other coaches. His 1978 Bullets earned the NBA championship, sharing the basketball and the glory as his style insists. They had six players average more than 10 points per game and eight players make major contributions. Center Wes Unseld scored only 7.6 points per game, but grabbed 11.9 rebounds per game and passed for 4.1 assists. The clearest evidence of Motta's coaching ability, however, was probably his resurrection of the Dallas Mavericks in 1994–1995. Called the "Mav-wrecks" the year before he took over, they had one of the worst seasons of any team in history and won only 13 games. With Motta and rookie point guard Jason Kidd, Dallas managed 36 victories and nearly made the playoffs.

The only outfit Jerry Tarkanian has been unable to beat in his coaching career has been the NCAA. His programs at Long Beach State and Nevada–Las Vegas were under near-constant scrutiny for suspected violations of recruiting rules, and twice they earned sanctions that kept them from playing in the NCAA Tournament.

Three years out of the game didn't affect Jerry Tarkanian when he returned to Fresno State in 1995 and led the Bulldogs to a winning season.

When Tark the Shark's teams were eligible to compete, they were a terror. At Nevada-Las Vegas, the Runnin' Rebels four times made the Final Four and won the 1990 NCAA title, but he left in 1992 after battling the NCAA's enforcement agents for nearly 20 years. He coached less than half a season in the NBA, then got the opportunity to return to college coaching when Fresno State, his alma mater, offered him a job in 1995.

"The thing I've found out that I missed the most was the association with the players," Tarkanian says. "I love just talking to them when they come by the office, talking to them about their problems and helping them out. A lot of them have baggage and have had tough backgrounds and experiences that other people can't relate to. Talking to them and helping them is what I missed the most."

Some of coaching's born winners settle comfortably into one place and stay in spite of all the opportunities that are thrown their way. "When you really look at college basketball and any program that sustains itself for a long time," says Mike Jarvis, coach at George Washington University, "the one common denominator is the coach."

They call Don Haskins "The Bear" and Clarence Gaines "Big House," but neither ever wanted to be as frightening as his nickname implies. Haskins, the coach at Texas–El Paso for thirty years, is among the top ten coaches in career victo-ries and has won nearly 70 percent of his games. Gaines is one of three coaches at any college level to win more than 800 games, and is a member of the Basketball Hall of Fame. He stayed at Winston-Salem, which played small college competition, from 1947 through 1993, even though he had offers to coach at the major college level.

Georgetown coach John Thompson has no menacing nickname, but he likes the idea that he intimidates others: reporters, opponents, and game officials. Thompson stands six feet ten inches (208cm) and weighs nearly 300 pounds (136kg), and is a former center with the Boston Celtics. He has been coach at Georgetown University since 1973, winning more than 500 games and the 1984 NCAA title.

Denny Crum left his assistant coaching job at UCLA to become head coach at the University of Louisville in 1971. He put the Cardinals into the Final Four in two of his first five seasons, proving he was a worthy successor to his mentor at UCLA, John Wooden. When Crum was offered that honor, he turned it down. "I had grown to love Louisville so much I didn't want to leave."

Louisville's basketball fans, and there are many, have had a bunch of reasons to love Crum. He has given them two NCAA titles and six trips to the Final Four. "I learned from the best and tried to put that to good use," Crum says. "I was able to recruit some good athletes that maybe weren't the best players coming in, but athletes with good attitudes that worked really hard who progressed. Those are the main things. There are all kinds of little things.

"Some teams aren't as talented as others, but they play together, and they all played their best at year's end. Sometimes it's not enough to win, but they are usually playing their best bas-ketball when it matters."

LEFT: Louisville coach Denny Crum gives some advice to forward Jason Osborne. OPPOSITE: Georgetown coach John Thompson has established one of the most successful programs in the NCAA and helped such players as Patrick Ewing and Alonzo Mourning develop into NBA superstars.

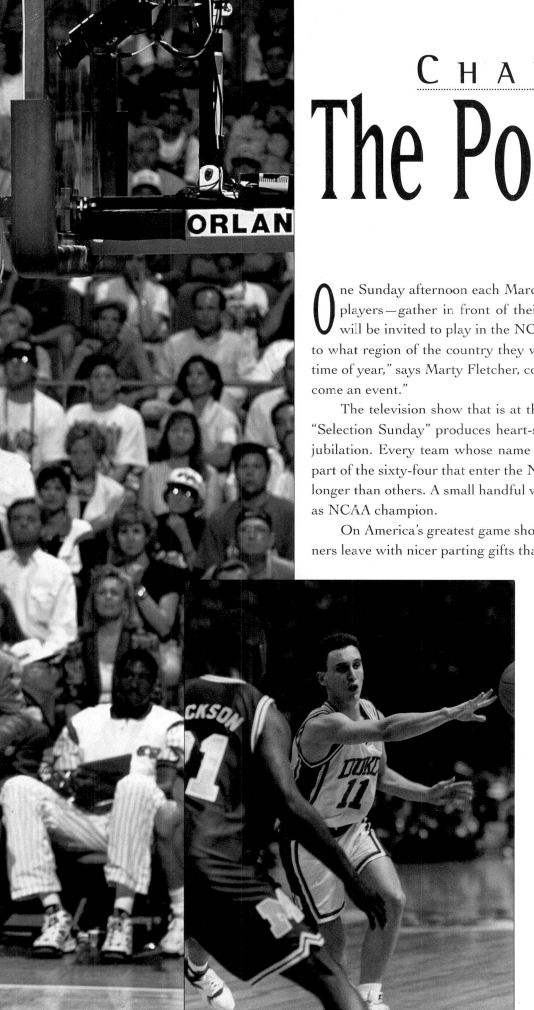

CHAPTER SIX

The Postseason

O ne Sunday afternoon each March, basketball fans—as well as coaches and players—gather in front of their televisions to learn which college teams will be invited to play in the NCAA Tournament, whom they will play, and to what region of the country they will be sent to compete. "It really is a great time of year," says Marty Fletcher, coach at Southwestern Louisiana. "It has become an event."

The television show that is at the core of what college basketball fans call "Selection Sunday" produces heart-stopping drama, anger and agony, joy and jubilation. Every team whose name is called in that half hour is pleased to be part of the sixty-four that enter the NCAA Tournament. Some will hang around longer than others. A small handful will last until the Final Four. One will finish as NCAA champion.

On America's greatest game show, there are no losers, but some of the winners leave with nicer parting gifts than the others.

"I don't want to compare it to a game show," says CBS-TV announcer Jim Nantz, who has broadcast the tournament for more than a decade. "But it's like suddenly being told: 'Hey, you're going to Salt Lake City, and while you're there, you're going to be playing the UCLA Bruins.'"

At every level of basketball, the postseason is different from all that has gone on before. In high schools and colleges, there is that threat of instant elimination inherent in a tournament format. One loss, and a team is done. Finished. No more basketball until the following autumn. In the NBA, there is the heightened intensity that results from knowing all the hard work that has gone into the six-month regular season could be wasted in one five- or seven-game series, and the increased antagonism that results from two teams trying to find ways to beat each other every other night for two weeks.

Mistakes are magnified. Every coach's decision is measured for its consequences.

LEFT: Orlando's Nick Anderson recovered from missing 4 late free throws in Game One of the 1995 NBA Finals to challenge Hakeem Olajuwon with this drive; but Houston won the title, and Anderson was stuck with that legacy. ABOVE: Duke's Bobby Hurley passes off in front of Michigan's Ray Jackson during the 1992 NCAA championship game.

ABOVE: A little failure can be a healthy ingredient in an NBA championship team, as Isiah Thomas and the Detroit Pistons proved by dropping a tough series to Boston in the 1987 playoffs then the 1988 Finals to Los Angeles before winning it all in 1989 and 1990. OPPOSITE: In his final game as a collegian, Michigan's Chris Webber dominated the inside game for nearly 40 minutes, but his last rebound turned into a moment he'll never completely escape: he called timeout when the Wolverines had none available, and North Carolina won the 1993 NCAA title.

Heroes are sorted from the ordinary players and those doomed to be goats.

How could Nick Anderson, a star guard for the Orlando Magic, miss 4 consecutive free throws when any one of them would have won the first game of the 1995 NBA finals for his team? He did, and the Magic were swept by the Houston Rockets. How could Isiah Thomas of the Detroit Pistons throw a careless inbounds pass in the 1987 playoffs that was so easy for the Boston Celtics' Larry Bird to steal? Bird passed to Dennis Johnson for a twisting layup, and the Celtics won that game and eventually the series before dropping the NBA finals to the Los Angeles Lakers. If Thomas hadn't led the Pistons to championships in 1989 and 1990, he might never have been permitted to forget that mistake.

The immense pressure of the postseason weighed heavily on Michigan All-American forward Chris Webber, who rebounded a missed North Carolina shot with his team trailing by a point in the closing seconds of the 1993 NCAA championship game, then desperately called time-out. His team had none, resulting in a technical foul that clinched the title for the Tar Heels. The postseason made college heroes of such players as guard Donald Williams, who shot North Carolina to the 1993 title in a moment of brilliance in an otherwise ordinary career, and Indiana's Keith Smart, who made the short jumper that gave the Hoosiers the 1987 NCAA championship by 1 point over Syracuse.

The series format in the NBA playoffs leads to fewer upsets and fewer unlikely stars; excellence has a way of establishing itself as there are more opportunities. And yet there are moments that leave fans gasping—some the work of such greats as Michael Jordan and Julius Erving, others from such unexpected sources as Los Angeles Lakers forward Elden Campbell, who helped Johnson push the team to a surprising appearance in the 1991 NBA finals.

In 1994, the Denver Nuggets were able to come from 2 games down in a first-round playoff series and win 3 in a row to stun the Seattle Super Sonics, who had the NBA's best regular-season record. At the end, Nuggets center Dikembe Mutombo celebrated as he lay on the court, unwilling and almost unable to get to his feet. He wanted to enjoy that moment as long as he could.

There still were more games to play—and, eventually for the Nuggets, a sudden, unhappy ending in the playoffs' next round. That is the postseason. Extraordinary excitement. Inordinate pressure. The best of what basketball has become.

Magic Johnson first emerged as a basketball star in leading Michigan State to the 1979 Final Four, where the Spartans destroyed Pennsylvania in the semifinals.

CBS announcer Jim Nantz, who has broadcast the Final Four on television for more than a decade, says no other sporting event in the U.S. has the same month-long hold on the audience as the NCAA Tournament. "March is owned by college basketball."

The Final Four is a goal that has been reached by nearly all of the game's legendary players: Indiana State's Larry Bird, Michigan State's Magic Johnson, James Worthy and Michael Jordan of North Carolina, Kareem Abdul-Jabbar of UCLA, and Wilt Chamberlain of Kansas. There were some greats who never made it, though: Shaquille O'Neal and Pete Maravich of LSU, and Walt Frazier of Southern Illinois.

"It's a big event, but I didn't realize how big until I got the chance to see it over the years," says former Memphis All-American Larry Finch, who scored 29 points while losing the 1973 title game to UCLA. "I didn't realize how big that one particular game was until it was long gone."

The first NCAA Tournament was played in 1939, with the final contest on March 27 at Patten Gymnasium in Evanston, Illinois. Dick Boughner played guard for Ohio State in that game, which the Buckeyes lost to Oregon by a 46–33 score. Back then, he considered it "just another game." It was an unknown tournament, and the Buckeyes weren't terribly excited about conquering all of college basketball. "In those days, your goal was to win the Big Ten, and to heck with everything else. Around comes this tournament—and who wanted to play another game?

There would be no way in the world I could ever conceive that this thing was going to develop into sixty-four teams playing several weeks to get it all done."

The major-college season starts with more than three hundred teams. Since 1985, sixty-four teams have made it to the tournament, nearly half earning their positions by winning conference championships. The rest are selected by a panel of athletic administrators who examine win-loss records, computer rankings, and other data from the regular season to determine the teams worthy of invitations. The nine-member committee is sequestered for four days

Michael Jordan made the Final Four just once during his college career, but nailed the game winning jumper for North Carolina in the 1982 title game.

at a hotel in Kansas City, Missouri, and spends all that time working on the selections. The announcement of the tournament pairings, televised live on CBS, is almost as much an event as the games themselves.

"It's a mentally exhausting process because you live it the entire time," says Kansas University athletic director Bob Frederick, who served two years as committee chairman. "Even in our free moments, which aren't very many, you're talking about it. Like at dinner, we've got three tele-

visions going, and you're talking about those games, so you just never get away from it. It's something I really look forward to, and when the thing is completed, you go, 'Whew!' You're glad to have that behind you."

The sixty-four teams that are chosen play a single-elimination tournament—at thirteen sites over three weekends—that occasionally squeezes out the best teams, but always produces remarkable drama. Tiny Manhattan College began the 1995 tournament by shocking a highly regarded Okla-

OPPOSITE: With a number of tournament records and two game-winning shots to put Duke in the Final Four, center Christian Laettner is widely considered the NCAA Tournament's greatest player. ABOVE: Togetherness helped lift UCLA to the 1995 title after two empty decades, the Bruins surviving an injury to star point guard Tyus Edney and the challenge of the defending champion Arkansas Razorbacks. RIGHT: Bill Walton was flawless in the 1973 final.

homa team. In 1993, Southern University ran talented Georgia Tech off the floor. The University of Richmond became an upset specialist, starting with a victory against Auburn in 1984, continuing with wins against Georgia Tech and Indiana in 1988, and finally scoring its most stunning triumph, a 73–69 decision against Syracuse in 1991. Richmond became the first team seeded fifteenth (out of sixteen teams in its region) to win a game in the tournament.

Other schools gained fame among basketball fans merely by coming close to such surprises. Princeton nearly upset Georgetown in 1989, losing by only 1 point. In 1986, Mississippi Valley State had number one Duke in a tight game until the closing minutes, losing by an 85–78 final score. Teams of this sort are accustomed to playing in gyms with smaller crowds and no television audiences, and arrive at the tournament hoping to achieve just one victory against a team like Kansas or Maryland.

Powers such as Duke, Arkansas, and North Carolina have reinforced their winning reputations by lasting into the Final Four more often than seems plausible, given the difficulty of surviving the "one-and-done" format. In 1980 and 1981, DePaul entered the tournament ranked number one and lost its first game both times. Five times between 1986 and 1994, the top-ranked team at the start of the tournament was unable to reach the Final Four. During that same stretch, however, coach Mike Krzyzewski led Duke to the Final Four seven times, the Blue Devils winning the championship in 1991 and 1992.

Only UCLA, which won the tournament ten times between 1964 and 1975 under coach John Wooden, produced a better run than Duke in tournament play. Jimmy Collins, who played guard for the New Mexico State team that lost to UCLA in the 1970 semifinals, says being part of the Final Four was wonderful except for the inevitability of defeat. "It's always been special. The only difference at that particular time was that you knew you would be in it with UCLA."

The Bruins' success in that period increased the pressure to win on the coaches who followed Wooden when he retired in 1975. It was so overwhelming that five coaches moved through UCLA in a matter of thirteen years before Jim Harrick took the job in 1988 and led the Bruins to a championship seven years later, at the Kingdome in Seattle in 1995.

He never really allowed himself to enjoy the victory over Arkansas, as it happened, even though UCLA was in command when most title games are still in doubt. After All-America forward Ed O'Bannon dunked to put the Bruins ahead by 11 with 30 seconds left, "I was more worried about us getting back on defense," Harrick says. "That's the way the tournament is. It's a scary thing. Winning it was a special moment, but you know, I didn't have much emotion because you're out of emotion. You've used it all. That three-week period is one of the most intense times I've ever been involved in."

UCLA's relatively one-sided victory against Arkansas was uncommon for NCAA title games. Between 1980 and 1994, the championship was decided by 6 points or less ten times, including four that turned in the final 10 seconds. In 1983, Lorenzo Charles of North Carolina State dunked an air ball from teammate Derek Whittenburg to defeat heavily favored Houston. In 1987, Indiana's Keith Smart nailed a fifteen-foot (4.5m) jumper with 4 seconds left to edge Syracuse. Michigan guard Rumeal Robinson made 2 free throws in the final seconds of overtime to push the Wolverines past Seton Hall. Strangest of all was in 1993, when Michigan center Chris Webber called a timeout the Wolverines did not have, an automatic technical foul that cost his team a chance at victory.

The singular beauty of the Final Four is that the joy (and occasional agony) of participating is shared among four teams and their supporters. The champion goes away happiest, with the best reason to boast, but any player who reaches the Final Four is bound to include that on his résumé. Corey Beck made it to the Final Four twice as an Arkansas point guard, in

ABOVE: Surrounded by stars like Grant Hill and Bobby Hurley, Coach Mike Krzyzewski was the center of attention in 1992, when Duke became the first NCAA team to repeat as champion since UCLA's run of seven consecutive titles ended in 1973. OPPOSITE: Kareem Abdul-Jabbar still was known as Lew Alcindor when he led UCLA to his third championship in three seasons with a win over Purdue.

Ed O'Bannon of 1994 UCLA (top) and James Worthy of 1992 North Carolina (above) were athletic power forwards who led their teams to championships and claimed the Most Outstanding Player award at the Final Four.

1994 and 1995. "It is one of the greatest feelings you can have, except for winning it."

When UCLA reached the 1995 Final Four with a victory in the West region final against Connecticut, Ed O'Bannon grabbed a portable video camera and recorded the traditional net-cutting ceremony from every possible angle, including the top rung of the ladder used to reach the rim. "I like to record things on tape that I am going to look back at later on and cherish, and this is definitely one of those things. The view from the ladder was the best of anything I ever had in my life."

Dynasties

The sporting world often expects teams that win championships to do the same thing again the next season. There is one very large problem. "Everything changes," says Denny Crum, head coach at the University of Louisville.

His Cardinals have twice won the NCAA Championship, in 1980 and 1986, and they didn't come close to repeating either time. In the 1981 season, they lost 7 of their first 9 games. In 1987, they became one of the few champions in recent years that failed to be invited back to the NCAA Tournament to defend their title.

Crum thus has a deepened understanding of all that makes even starting a sports dynasty difficult, let alone sustaining one. "Your self-motivation changes...now you have a tendency to coast at times. The chemistry of things; kids get a year older. Some of them, their career's running out. They haven't had a chance to play a lot. Last year, it's okay; this year, it's not. You may have internal strife, and all the kids' family and personal lives are different this year than they were a year ago. There are all kinds of things that change, even if the personnel doesn't."

The definition of the dynasty has changed in sports. It used to be that a team had to win a number of titles in a row to stake that claim, but because of free agency and the instant wealth that can change a player's attitude toward hard work, now a team that wins two, like the Detroit Pistons in 1989 and 1990, might have a claim to being a dynasty. Certainly the Chicago Bulls, with their three titles from 1991 to 1993, can stake such a claim. In college basketball, where money is not a consideration but where the best players are spread among more teams, Duke had a sort of dynasty going even before winning its first NCAA title. The Blue Devils reached the coveted Final Four a total of four times in five years before winning their first of two consecutive championships. In all, Duke's run of Final Four trips extended to seven in nine seasons.

There was a time when the Boston Celtics ruled professional basketball and UCLA ruled college basketball, and that was just the way it was. The Celtics won eleven NBA championships in the thirteen years between 1957 and 1969, with center Bill Russell the primary ingredient on all of those teams. UCLA's cast of players changed four times, but coach John Wooden remained in place, as the Bruins won ten NCAA titles between 1964 and 1975.

The Celtics' record in playoff games during their run was 108–59, a .647 winning percentage that is amazing considering they were always playing the best teams in the league at that stage. The Celtics dominated the NBA by playing a consummate brand of team defense and a precise fast-break offense. Opponents could only stop the break by first solving that tough Boston defense and putting the ball through the basket, which meant the Celts would have to take the time to inbound the ball.

Their seamless, unselfish style made it less important for players to play specific roles. John Havlicek played both small forward and shooting guard, bringing the same hard-charging

ABOVE: Joe Dumars passes between two Portland defenders during the 1989–1990 NBA Finals, which the Pistons won for their second consecutive championship. LEFT: The Louisville Cardinals celebrate after winning the West Division of the NCAA Tournament in 1986 to advance to the Final Four. The Cardinals went on to win the championship that year, their second title in five years.

style to both positions. Guards Sam Jones and K.C. Jones were interchangeable in the backcourt.

"The Celtics, as a rule, just played, and you had to be able to play with whatever combination was on the floor," says Quinn Buckner, who grew up watching the tail end of the Boston dynasty on TV and was a guard for the Celts' 1984 NBA champions. "They were the team I always felt I could be a part of."

Of the players on those Boston teams, eight have been elected to the Hall of Fame: Bob Cousy, K.C. Jones, Sam Jones, Tom Heinsohn, John Havlicek, Bill Russell, and Frank Ramsey. Coach Red Auerbach is in there as well. All of those men owe a debt to Russell, considered the best defensive center in the history of basketball, and perhaps the greatest winner in modern team sports. Not by coincidence, the Celtics' dynasty began the day Russell

UCLA's 1964 NCAA championship was the first of 10 coach John Wooden would claim.

After center Bill Russell joined the Boston Celtics for the 1957 season, they began to dominate their sport like no professional franchise before or since, winning eleven NBA championships during his playing career.

signed on to the team in 1956, and ended when he retired after winning the 1969 title. Russell was coach of that team, and his best idea was to play himself more than any other player. He pulled in 19.3 rebounds per game but scored only 9.9 points, the one and only time in his career when he did not average in double figures. The team he drove to the championship that year was probably the weakest of any Celtics team to win it; the team finished fourth in the regular season but edged the Los Angeles Lakers by a 108–106 score in the final match of a seven-game series.

The UCLA dynasty began with its 1964 championship team, led by guards Walt Hazzard and Gail Goodrich and six-foot-five-inch (195cm) center Keith Erickson, and continued as coach Wooden was able to attract dominant centers Lew Alcindor and Bill Walton.

"I remember the first time we played them, we walked into that gym and instead of us doing our warm-ups, we spent most of the time looking at [Alcindor]," says Jimmy Collins, a guard for New Mexico State's 1970 Final Four team, which lost to UCLA in the semifinals. "We played UCLA too many times. John Wooden, of course, made them great."

As was the case with Russell and the Celtics, UCLA's phenomenal success ended the day Wooden retired. The

Horace Grant and the Chicago Bulls saw their mini-dynasty end when Michael Jordan briefly retired and spent a summer playing baseball.

Keeping stars like Grant Hill in school and out of the NBA Draft for four years enabled Duke to reach the Final Four seven times between 1986 and 1994.

Bruins won the 1975 NCAA title in Wooden's final game; they did not win the tournament again until 1995.

In the nearly two decades in between, only one college team repeated as champion: Duke, in 1991 and 1992. No matter how many times the reigning champion returned with most or all of its regular players, that team failed to win it again. In fact, only five made it back to the Final Four, and most were eliminated from the NCAA Tournament by the second round.

The NBA went through seventeen years without a repeat champion, but as long-term contracts and a cap on salaries kept players in place for three- and four-year periods, it became more common. Four consecutive teams repeated, and the Chicago Bulls, led by superstar guard Michael Jordan, became only the third team in the league's history to win three in a row, to "three-peat," as the achievement is now known.

After the Bulls won their third in a row, they appeared at a downtown Chicago rally and talked openly of doing it a fourth time. Forward Horace Grant promised fans if they offered the same support as in the first three title years, "I guarantee another…four-peat." Said Jordan: "Certainly, destiny shall be back here for the fourth time."

It turned out Jordan wasn't even back for the fourth time. He temporarily retired, walking away from basketball during the 1993–1994 season and spending his time playing minor league baseball. The Bulls made the playoffs, but lost in the second round.

CHAPTER SEVEN

Overtime

ABOVE: To see four of the game's greatest scorers on the same play—Adrian Dantley, Julius Erving, Kareem Abdul-Jabbar, and Moses Malone—is almost a routine occurence in the annual NBA All-Star Game. OPPOSITE: Grant Hill, shown here floating up for a dunk while Shawn Kemp and Hakeem Olajuwon look on, has been voted to the all-star team in both of his first two seasons as a pro.

The All-Star Game

It has been called the ultimate pick-up game, and it is clear that this is true because those who aren't chosen for the NBA All-Star Game walk away with hurt feelings and diminished egos. No one appreciates being ignored when sides are chosen for a friendly game of basketball, least of all those who consider themselves among the best in the sport.

It happens every year that players complain about being passed over, and then insist it's not a big deal and they'd rather have the three days off. It might be Cliff Robinson of the Trail Blazers or Dikembe Mutombo of the Nuggets, but no one enjoys being left out.

With only a five-thousand-dollar difference between the paychecks for the players on the winning team and those on the losing end, those who do make it take the ac-

tual game less seriously than being selected. It's being there that matters. "Anytime you get a chance to play in an All-Star Game, there's a lot of people that watch that type of thing, and there's a lot of exposure you wouldn't normally get," says retired Indiana Pacers guard Don Buse. "It turned out to be a good experience and it had to help my career."

Buse played in one NBA All-Star Game, in 1977, and was a late addition because Portland center Bill Walton was injured and could not play. Although Buse was not a big scorer, he was among the leaders in assists and steals, as he had been in the American Basketball Association before the two leagues became one.

"That was the first year of the merger, so a lot of players from the ABA were getting seen on TV for the first

time," Buse says. "There were probably announcers for that game that didn't know much about me at all."

In fact, the announcers didn't have much reason to notice Buse, with Julius Erving, Bob McAdoo, and Kareem Abdul-Jabbar putting on such a spectacular show. The 1977 All-Star Game was perhaps the most influential in the forty-five-year history of the event. With Erving bringing his flare for the game to a wide national audience and demonstrating all the airborne possibilities of basketball, it was the game that made fans look forward to the All-Stars sharing the court. McAdoo scored 30 points, Abdul-Jabbar had 18 for the winning side, and Phoenix guard Paul Westphal scored the two baskets that clinched a 125–124 victory for the West All-Stars, but Erving captivated the audience and captured the MVP award.

Thereafter, the All-Star Game became a focal point of the NBA season, and the MVP trophy a goal of all who were invited to play. The selection of starters for the game had been opened to fan balloting in 1975, following the course set by major league baseball. By 1984, the league had expanded the All-Star event to a full weekend, with a game between retired legends and a slam-dunk contest played the day before the main event. In 1986, a three-point shooting contest was added and in 1994 a rookie game replaced the legends game.

"The All-Star Game is prestigious to the NBA players," says Orlando guard Anfernee Hardaway, who was voted to the starting lineup in his second season. "Making it in my second year meant a lot, made me feel like I'd accomplished a lot of things."

The fan voting produced a truly memorable All-Star Game in 1992, when Magic Johnson was nominated to a spot on the West starting lineup even though he had retired from the game before the season began, after learning he had contracted HIV, the virus believed to cause AIDS. Johnson played in his eleventh and final All-Star Game and led the West to a 40-point victory with 9 assists and 25 points. He was named MVP. Johnson, explaining that he missed the passion and togetherness of playing pro basketball, said he "wanted to go out this way…I will cherish this for the rest of my life, whatever happens."

Because defense is not a priority, the All-Star Game can serve as the stage for such amazing offensive performances as Michael Jordan's 40-point explosion in the 1988 game at Chicago Stadium, his home court. Because team play is not a priority, things can get a little ragged. John Stockton of the Utah Jazz committed 12 turnovers in the 1989 game in Houston, which is about what he'll let loose in 4 games during the regular season.

Brilliant passing made John Stockton (left, top) of the Utah Jazz an All-Star Game regular, along with Magic Johnson of the Lakers and Michael Jordan of the Bulls (left). Jordan and Johnson play different positions and don't commonly face each other on the court, but the relaxed atmosphere of the All-Star Game allows them to try some one-on-one encounters. OPPOSITE: In 1986, near the end of his career, Julius Erving was still an All-Star attraction.

INTERNATIONAL EXPLOSION

The United States has had trouble in recent years selling its automobiles and electronic gadgets to foreign markets, but there has been an abundance of customers for one of its fresher exports: basketball.

The game was popular only regionally in the U.S. just a few decades ago, but is now reaching to all corners of the world. The NBA has fans in just about every nation, and those countries are now beginning to play basketball at a level high enough to produce NBA-caliber players. Athletes from Australia, China, and Israel have been stars in U.S. colleges. Far from the time in 1985 when forward Georgi Glouchkov, the Bulgarian Banger, was viewed as a novelty during his one season with the Phoenix Suns, Sarunas Marciulionis of Lithunia, Detlef Schrempf of Germany, and Rik Smits of The Netherlands have been excellent NBA players throughout this decade.

At the 1992 Olympic Games in Barcelona, Spain, the U.S. Olympic squad that will forever be known as the Dream Team was inundated by attention from fans and reporters. A press conference featuring team members drew one thousand media representatives to ask questions. The questions were strange at times, but demonstrated the worldwide reverence accorded the NBA stars. As did the fact that some journalists applauded the players. "How do you feel to be called as a god?" one Japanese reporter asked Chicago Bulls star Michael Jordan. The hotel where the players stayed had to be manned with a vast security force. Mostly, the security was needed not to protect the players from vacationing U.S. citizens enthralled by their presence, but rather from fans from around the world who don't often come in contact with NBA players and were attempting to take advantage of this opportunity.

Evidence of basketball's exploding worldwide popularity is available in many areas. The NBA has a vast international marketing arm to help spread the sale of league-related merchandise, with offices in Switzerland, Australia, Hong Kong, and Tokyo. The NBA Finals in 1995 were seen on television in 160 countries. The league has sponsored regular-season games in Japan, and the McDonald's Open international tournament includes teams from the NBA and various foreign leagues. League commissioner David Stern has turned down U.S. cities wishing to establish expansion teams to add two clubs in Canada, the Toronto Raptors and the Vancouver Grizzlies, and remains interested in placing a team in Mexico City.

"We're not going to be putting teams in Europe to play in our league," Stern says, "but the growth of TV allows people around the world to see our game...the world has gotten to know more about our game and our players."

In the world-famous Harrod's department store, in the Knightsbridge section of London, Shawn Kemp's Seattle SuperSonics jersey and Magic Johnson's Lakers jersey hang on the same sale rack as uniform tops for soccer clubs West Ham United and Leeds. U.S. astronaut Hoot Gibson of the space shuttle Atlantis carried a T-shirt bearing the logo of the 1995 NBA champion Houston Rockets into space with him and presented it as a gift to Russian cosmonaut Anatoly Solovyev when the two met in the space station Mir.

Former American college stars can be paid more than $1 million dollars to compete in European leagues, and those players often have their living expenses paid for them as well. Former University of Tennessee guard Tony White and Walter Berry of St. John's, the 1986 college player of the year, are among those U.S. players who have been content to accept the comfortable living afforded by playing ball overseas rather than scrape out an existence on the fringes of the NBA.

John Tarkas, a sports agent in Athens, Greece, who places U.S. players with teams in the Greek league, says players chosen in the second round of the NBA draft are often interested in the money available in Europe. "But to get a rookie, you're walking a fine line, because teams expect American players to carry them."

European fans can be even less understanding and more demanding than their counterparts in the U.S. And the international rules allow for a more physical style of play than is found at American colleges. Thus, some players who aren't ready for the NBA at age twenty-two or twenty-three have used the European leagues to prepare them from a physical and psychological standpoint. Antonio Davis, who began his career in Greece after averaging just 9.2 points in four college seasons at Texas-El Paso, is one example. "If he had stayed on an NBA bench," says Tarkas, "maybe he wouldn't have developed his game so much."

Not all of the best players in Europe are American. It used to be that players from outside the U.S. were uniformly excellent

When he led the Soviet Union to the 1988 Olympic gold medal, guard Sarunas Marciulionis proved he was worthy of a position in the NBA. He has played with the Golden State Warriors, Seattle Sonics, and, most recently, the Sacramento Kings.

shooters but stiff and mechanical in their play, ignorant of the creative possibilities available in basketball. Not any longer. Arvidas Sabonis is a seven-foot (213cm) center from Lithuania with a lethal shooting touch who was long coveted by the NBA's Portland Trail Blazers, but who spent most of his career playing in Spain. Forward Toni Kukoc of Croatia chose to play in Europe for the early part of his career before eventually deciding to test himself with the NBA's Chicago Bulls. "It's a change in the way I play a little bit. Before, I handled the ball more," says Kukoc, who stands six feet eleven inches (210cm) but played a great deal at point guard before entering the NBA. "Playing in the NBA, playing with the Bulls—everything is here. There's a lot of good things."

Toni Kukoc of Croatia was a controversial addition to the Chicago Bulls when he joined the team after a productive career in Europe, but he proved the doubters among his new teammates wrong and became an offensive force.

The versatility that has made Detlef Schrempf a productive NBA player is typical of European players, who emphasize shooting and passing skills over running and dunking.

Kukoc was an integral part of the team that, prior to the Dream Team, might have been the greatest ever assembled for an international competition. Although the 1960 U.S. Olympic team had eventual Hall of Famers Jerry Lucas, Jerry West, and Oscar Robertson, and the 1984 team had Patrick Ewing, Michael Jordan, and Chris Mullin, all those players were barely out of their teens, had not yet played professional ball, and were together only a short time before rampaging toward their gold medals. The team from Yugoslavia that won the 1990 Olympic World Championship and 1990 Goodwill Games featured Kukoc, center Vlade Divac of the Los

Angeles Lakers, the late Drazen Petrovic, who was an all-star shooting guard for the New Jersey Nets, and power forward Dino Radja, who later joined the Boston Celtics.

The Yugoslavs played together seamlessly and selflessly, sharing the basketball and the glory as they destroyed the competition in those two summer tournaments, including a U.S. entry that included future NBA stars Alonzo Mourning, Billy Owens, and Kenny Anderson. Ironically, the team was torn apart when their country was split in pieces before the 1992 Olympics, when they might have presented a challenge to the Dream Team.

"For years, European pro players have been in the Olympics and nothing has been said," point guard Magic Johnson said during the '92 Games. "Now, we play and everybody makes a big deal of it."

This is one instance in basketball in which the game isn't the thing, it's the show. If three attempts at dazzling passes roll over the end line, it hardly matters. If one leads to a spectacular slam by someone like Shawn Kemp, that is what is remembered.

"The All-Star appearances are fun," says former Golden State guard Jeff Mullins, who made it three consecutive years, from 1969 to 1971. "The things I remember best about the All-Star games, though, is that you get to socialize with guys you're used to competing against. That's what made it special for me."

The Olympics

Jeff Mullins played in the Final Four, in the NBA All-Star Game, and in the NBA Finals. He was an All-American in his senior season at Duke. He was part of the 1975 NBA championship won by the Golden State Warriors. All of that was a bonus. "I think the only long-range goal I ever set for myself in basketball was to try to make the Olympic team." And he did, winning a gold medal in Tokyo in 1964.

Mullins was in it for the travel as well as the honor. When he left for Tokyo, he'd never before been out of the country. With basketball becoming more organized and sophisticated, and more global, players get the opportunity to play in international competition while still in high school, and to tour the U.S. for high school games and summer tournaments. "For me, that was an adventure," Mullins says. "Some of these kids, they've probably been to Paris with their AAU teams by the time they're in the ninth grade, and they'd been to Vegas five times. It was a dream come true for me."

Before there was a Dream Team, players dreamed of representing their country and defending its basketball tradition against those who would dare present a challenge. That is still an honor, but now there is no challenge. In 1992, the U.S. team that featured Michael Jordan, Magic Johnson, and Larry Bird annihilated its Olympic opponents, including a 32-point victory in the gold medal game. The players who are part of the 1996 U.S. Olympic team view their selections, at least in part, as a status thing.

"It's the ultimate," says Anfernee Hardaway, who was chosen for the '96 U.S. team, along with forwards Grant Hill and Glenn Robinson and center Shaquille O'Neal. "You can have guys make the NBA here or there, for a couple months or a couple weeks or even an entire career. But not everybody can make the Olympic team. I'll always cherish it."

A six-foot-four-inch (193cm) guard, Mullins joined with such players as Bill Bradley of Princeton University, Luke Jackson of Pan American, and Walt Hazzard of UCLA to win the gold medal for the United States. That was hardly a shock. The U.S. won every gold medal awarded—and every basketball game it played—from the

ABOVE: Magic Johnson didn't get the opportunity to play in the Olympics as a collegian, but interrupted his retirement in 1992 to be a part of the first Dream Team of NBA pros. OPPOSITE: Karl Malone and Christian Laettner helped lead the United States to a laughably easy victory in the qualifying tournament that put the Dream Team in the Barcelona Olympics.

time the game was introduced to the Olympics in 1936 until the final match of the 1972 Games in Munich, Germany.

"I think everyone knew that basketball was our sport," Mullins says. "I can't remember it being an unbelievable pressure to win, because I think we felt we were better, knew we were better—even though I don't think our team was particularly strong, as strong as the 1960 team."

The 1960 team included future Hall of Fame members Jerry West, Oscar Robertson, and Jerry Lucas, but it didn't matter if the players were as widely respected as Bill Russell, who played center for the U.S. team in 1956 after leading San Francisco to consecutive NCAA championships, or as little known as Spencer Haywood. He made the U.S. team in 1968 and became a star while only nineteen years old, before he'd played at the University of Detroit. Many of the best college players, including Lew Alcindor of UCLA, chose not to join the team as a protest against racial discrimination. Haywood averaged 16 points and became the key to the U.S. victory in Mexico City.

Whoever was on the roster, the U.S. won. Until Munich. The game that changed the course of worldwide bas-

ketball almost wasn't played because of a terrorist attack in the athletes' village that killed eleven members of the Israeli Olympic team. When it was decided that the game should go on, it was played more than once.

The 1972 United States team did not have an abundance of the game's top college stars. Only one of that season's first-team All-Americans was on the team, Ed Ratleff of Long Beach State, as coach Hank Iba preferred superior defensive players. The U.S. had only one close game on the way to the final, though, and arrived with a 62 game winning streak in Olympic competition. Against the Soviet Union, the American team played what is surely the most bizarre game in basketball's history.

Far behind for much of the game, the U.S. rallied to a 1-point lead in the final seconds after guard Doug Collins stole the ball, was fouled on a layup, and made 2 free throws. The Soviet team tossed the ball inbounds and time

expired, but its coaches ran onto the floor protesting the fact that time had been called. The officials lost authority over the game as Dr. R. William Jones, director of the International Basketball Federation (FIBA), ordered the timekeeper to place three seconds back on the clock. After the timeout, the Soviets inbounded again, and again failed to score. And again, Jones ordered three seconds to be placed on the clock. This time, Ivan Edeshko of the U.S.S.R. completed a pass to teammate Aleksander Belov, who bullied through U.S. defenders Kevin Joyce and Jim Forbes for a basket that gave his team a 51–50 victory and the gold medal.

The official protests lodged by the U.S. were denied. The silver medals the American players earned were also refused. They sat in a bank vault, unclaimed. The team did not show up for the medal ceremony, at which the Soviet national anthem was played instead of the "Star-Spangled Banner." Collins continues to insist he'll never accept his silver medal. Although he claims to have lost any bitterness about what happened, he still feels a sting when he

Bill Russell's (above) strong defensive play as a center with the 1956 gold medalists set the standard for Patrick Ewing (right), who threw up a roadblock for Germany's Uwe Blab during a U.S. victory in the 1984 Games. Ewing's team included Michael Jordan, Chris Mullin, and Sam Perkins and is considered one of the best to have represented the United States in the Olympics. It was also the last team of college players to win a gold medal, with the 1988 team claiming a bronze medal, and the nation switching to NBA players for the 1992 Games.

Adrian Dantley was the leading scorer on the 1976 U.S. Olympic team, which restored the United States to international supremacy but was denied the opportunity to avenge the bitter defeat the U.S.S.R. inflicted four years earlier.

Michael Jordan is one of the few players in United States history to win two gold medals in basketball, having competed in Los Angeles in 1984 and Barcelona in 1992. He declined an opportunity to join the 1996 team, saying other players should be given the opportunity.

watches the Olympics and sees other U.S. athletes accepting gold medals. He wanted that experience.

Although this was one of the lowest moments in the history of American basketball, it seemed to have a profound and positive effect on the growth of the game around the world. Four years later, an excellent U.S. team that included such All-Americans as forwards Scotty May of Indiana, Adrian Dantley of Notre Dame and North Carolina guard Phil Ford defeated Puerto Rico by a point and struggled to pull away from Yugoslavia in the gold-medal game before winning by 21 points. It was clear the gap was closing. In 1988, it slammed shut. The U.S.S.R. beat the United States fair and square in the semifinals, 82–76, with future Seattle SuperSonics guard Sarunas Marciulionis starring for the winners. The Soviets left Seoul, Korea, with gold medals, the U.S. with bronze.

That was the last year that the U.S. was bound by international rules to use only amateur players, who came mostly from college teams. The following spring, FIBA voted by an overwhelming margin—with the U.S. dissenting—to have open competition. That meant NBA players

like Patrick Ewing and Karl Malone could play in the Olympics. Basketball experts in other countries felt the only way to catch up with the best players was to compete against them.

Despite some criticism from commentators and Cuban President Fidel Castro, who said the U.S. used NBA players "to show off their supremacy and arrogance," the United States decided to send its Dream Team to Barcelona in 1992. The team won 8 games by an average of 44 points. Before the first game, Angola coach Victorino de Silva Cunha admitted, "We can't beat the U.S.A. It is impossible. I'm not a crazy coach." The U.S. won by 68 points.

There never really has been agreement about whether the Dream Team was constructed because recent U.S. efforts in international basketball had failed or because this was an opportunity to spread the message of NBA excitement. When the U.S. claimed the gold medal, Jordan said U.S. citizens could "be proud of our basketball program again."

Larry Bird, though, wasn't even sure how proud he should be of himself. "I dreamed of playing in the

Olympics as a young kid, but when you win by 50 points every game, I think it takes away from it. When my kids are grown, I can say I played in the Olympics and won it."

The Women's Game

In 1995, the most popular basketball team on campus at the University of Connecticut was not coach Jim Calhoun's Huskies, who won the Big East Conference and were among the last eight standing in the NCAA Tournament. It was not the Boston Celtics or Orlando Magic or some other distant collection of NBA stars.

The most popular basketball team at UConn that winter had no one who could dunk and no one headed to the National Basketball Association. Connecticut's Lady Huskies sold out their home-court arena and captivated their state because they had become the best at their game, and because their game had grown to the point where that achievement could be appreciated.

The Lady Huskies finished that season 35–0, won the NCAA Championship, and became so widely recognized that their star, forward Rebecca Lobo, was asked to appear on David Letterman's CBS talk show. The sudden surge in the acceptance of women's basketball involved a number of factors that were peculiar to the Connecticut program, but also reflected the gradual growth of the sport from its true inception only two decades earlier.

"Everybody notices it's a much more athletic game today, a stronger game," says Anne Donovan, a center who was among the earliest women to be elected to the Basketball Hall of Fame. "It's what's happened off the court that led to this. We have better coaches, much better coaches, who reach girls at a young age. You were fortunate years ago if you got a decent coach. Girls understand now that this is a sport for young women, and you can be good at it. It's become a more attractive thing for girls to do."

When Nancy Lieberman was growing up in New York City in the early 1970s, she didn't play because she might one day receive an athletic scholarship for college or play in the Olympic Games (those goals were largely unavailable then, even to the few young girls who seemed interested), she played because she fell in love with the game. Now known as Nancy Lieberman-Kline, she played so much and so well that she became one of the sport's premier players.

"I was a creature of my environment. I played every single day: one-on-one, two-on-two. I never played against a girl until my sophomore year in high school. I knew I wanted to be the best basketball player in the world. I don't know why at ten years old you know this, but I was fortunate I understood what my goals were. Today, there are huge carrots dangling in front of athletes, and it makes working a heck of a lot easier. Twenty-five years ago, my reward was, 'You're a tomboy. Why are you

ABOVE: As the star of Connecticut's undefeated national champions in 1995, Rebecca Lobo attained a regional and national prominence uncommon among female basketball players.
OPPOSITE: The 1995 clash between Tennessee and Connecticut propelled the growth of women's basketball.

doing this? You're embarrassing the family.' I wasn't mugging, stealing, or taking drugs. I was playing a game that I loved that I felt was very healthy for me."

Basketball can be forced on youngsters who grow tall, but Donovan said she would have played the game even if she hadn't reached six feet eight inches (203cm). She was the youngest of eight children, her siblings providing the competition, and she had a basket in her backyard where she learned to play. "We had lots of energy, and that's how we got things settled if we had a problem: take it out to the basketball court. I loved the game and I loved to play. I have no idea how far I would have gone, but I would have been a player no matter how tall I was."

Women's basketball has existed in various forms almost since the game was invented in the 1890s by James Naismith. They played the sport as it was designed to be played until 1921, when some observers judged the game to be too rough for women and too taxing physically. A couple of different variations developed to alleviate those concerns, the most popular of which cut the court in half and put three players for each team at either end, with no one allowed to cross the center line. That meant some

OPPOSITE: Dawn Staley's superior point-guard play at Virginia helped her join the first U.S. women's Dream Team. ABOVE: Basketball was always ideal for women, but it took decades for their game to be established. RIGHT: Guard Dena Head was drawn to the high level of play in the Southeastern Conference.

players were never allowed to shoot and had to be content as defensive and rebounding specialists. That game was most popular in Iowa, where high school girls annually played their six-on-six game before capacity crowds during the state championship tournament. It wasn't until the 1990s that the six-player game died.

Women's basketball, otherwise, was largely dormant until the U.S. Congress passed a law known as Title IX in 1972, which mandated that all institutions receiving federal funds eliminate discrimination based on race and sex. That led to the formation of more women's athletic teams in high schools and colleges, providing more opportunities to play, better pay for coaches (leading to better coaches entering the sport), and a greater acceptance of athletics as a worthwhile pursuit for females. All this prompted the NCAA, which previously had not dealt in women's athletics, to begin sponsoring a basketball championship beginning in 1982, with Louisiana Tech beating Cheyney State for the title. However, fan interest and support increased at an even slower pace.

Several attempts at forming a major women's professional league in the United States failed, but that could have been predicted by examining attendance for college programs. It took eleven years, from 1982 until 1993, for average NCAA women's attendance to climb above one thousand per game. Even many of the best teams struggled to attract the same crowds as middling men's programs, and television networks were reluctant to spend money and air time on a sport that appeared to lack a sufficient following.

The best women's basketball could do in that regard was to generate one star player every few years. There were Lieberman, Donovan, and UCLA's Ann Meyers in the late 1970s, then Cheryl Miller of Southern California in the 1980s. It was a measure of the sport's progress that Meyers was widely known as the brother of David Meyers, the center on the UCLA men's team that won the 1975 NCAA championship, whereas a decade later Cheryl Miller was far better known than her brother, Reggie, when she was still an active player and he was playing college basketball at UCLA.

"When I played—and I say this with all humility—I was so much better when I came into college than so many of my teammates," Lieberman says. "I played like a boy, whereas today there is an abundance of players who play like boys." Even the disappearance of that comparison can be taken as an indication that women's basketball has grown. Lieberman still considers it to be a compliment, but she is one of the players who has made it unnecessary. Now, a player like Sheryl Swoopes, who led Texas Tech to the 1993 NCAA title, can be compared to Cheryl Miller. Dawn Staley, point guard for the 1996 U.S. Olympic team, is compared to Lieberman.

"I don't think a lot of the women playing years ago gave of themselves because I don't think they saw where it was going to take them," says Geno Auriemma, coach at

Cheryl Miller was so gifted and agile she came to be viewed as the best female player in U.S. history, leading Southern California to the NCAA title and winning a gold medal in the Olympics. She was voted into the Naismith Memorial Basketball Hall of Fame as soon as she became eligible.

Connecticut. "Administrations at the colleges, getting two hundred people at a game, wondered the same. And I think all that has changed. You can sell out. You can market the program. There's an audience for it. I don't think there was an audience for it back then because I don't think the game was good enough."

Average attendance at women's college games increased by 55 percent between 1991 and 1993. Connecticut's sudden impact on women's basketball came partly as the result of its challenge to the game's establishment, which includes such schools as Texas, Stanford, Virginia, and Tennessee. "Now," Donovan says, "there are so many competitive Division I teams that the Top 20 changes every week. It used to be you could always bank on Louisiana Tech, Tennessee, Old Dominion. Goodness knows it's changed, and we needed that."

Tennessee's Lady Vols have been a powerful basketball program for years, and were ranked number one in the nation upon arriving at UConn for a showdown game in the winter of 1995 that was televised nationally by the ESPN cable network. Auriemma compared that game, which his team won, to the famous UCLA–Houston game that was played at the Astrodome in 1968 and helped propel men's college basketball toward the popularity it enjoys today. Not a year had passed since that Tennessee–Connecticut game when ESPN announced it would televise a 64-game schedule of women's basketball on its main network and its subsidiary ESPN2. That was more than double the number of games that had been on the two networks before.

"Had they won, it would have been just another win for the number one team," Auriemma says. "Because we won and the way the fans reacted, I think that set the stage for the idea that, 'I hope those two get the chance to play again.' And then we did." Connecticut won the second time, also, in the title game of the NCAA Tournament.

The Lady Huskies' unbeaten record added to the excitement surrounding the team, and it helped that UConn was in the Northeast. The team began getting regular coverage in the *New York Times* and on the ESPN all-sports cable network, whose office is located in Bristol, Connecticut. ESPN featured the first UConn–Tennessee game and some early-round games in the NCAA Tournament in 1995; the network now has a long-term contract to broadcast the entire tournament.

Most of the game's pioneers believe that affiliation will help lift women's basketball to a higher level of interest and attention. At least as important is the formation of the first full-time U.S. women's Olympic team, which was selected one year before the 1996 Games so that it could play and practice together to prepare for the competition. Each player received a fifty-thousand-dollar salary, and the schedule permitted the most talented female players to be exposed to all areas of the country.

Donovan believes this may soon lead to the formation of a professional league, one of her fondest hopes for the game she loves. Lieberman is not thinking quite so big at the moment. Her goal is simpler: 'It's that you would be able to name the top twenty women's players in the country," Lieberman says. "We need more exposure, more marquee names. We've always had that one player—Anne Donovan, Sheryl Swoopes, or Lisa Leslie—and she gets all the attention. But you know there's more than one player out there.

"We're not the men. We don't profess to play the way men do, but women's basketball is a real fun game."

A Buzzer-Beater

Arkansas basketball fans call it "The Shot," as though they are the only fans who have a shot they call The Shot. Theirs was not the most dramatic, not the longest, not the most difficult, but it is theirs just the same, and Razorback fans will always be grateful to Scotty Thurman for what it meant to them.

There was slightly less than a minute left to play in the 1994 NCAA Championship game between Arkansas and Duke when forward Dwight Stewart caught the ball at the top of the key, not certain what play to make as the 35-second clock began to expire. He hesitated, then fumbled the ball. At that point, he could only think to get rid of it. Stewart found Thurman open to his right and passed the ball.

Thurman knew exactly what to do. As Duke forward Tony Lang ran toward him, trying to cause a distraction, Thurman calmly launched a three-point shot over Lang's hand that slammed through the basket to break a 70–70 tie and give Arkansas a 3-point lead to clinch the school's first national championship.

"I don't really think about it any, unless I'm asked about it," Thurman says. "The shot really didn't change my life any. It's something I'm proud of, but I'll probably be prouder of it when I get older."

The last-second shot is basketball's defining moment, the instant when a loser becomes a winner and a winner becomes a loser. Few other sports present so many opportunities for late-game drama. A team can hold the lead for the duration of the game, but if its opponent is allowed to stay too close, that lead can change hands for good just before the final buzzer sounds.

In an incredible 1995 NBA playoff game between the Indiana Pacers and Orlando Magic, the two teams traded seemingly decisive jump shots four times in the final 13 seconds, until Indiana center Rick Smits drew seven-foot-one-inch (215cm) Tree Rollins of Orlando off-balance with a pump-fake, swishing a twelve-footer (3.7m) to win the game with no time left. College fans recall another Arkansas player, U.S. Reed, heaving in a fifty-foot (15.4m) shot at the

Scotty Thurman will always be known at Arkansas for clinching the 1994 NCAA title.

buzzer to eliminate defending champion Louisville from the 1981 NCAA Tournament. In the pros, there was Chicago Bulls guard John Paxson's three-point shot with 3.9 seconds left to defeat the Phoenix Suns, 99–98, in the sixth and deciding game of the 1993 NBA Finals.

The Bulls were trailing by 2 points and needed only a dunk or layup to tie, but they gambled on Phoenix expecting them to play for the tie. Forward Horace Grant accepted a pass inside, then fired the ball to Paxson at the left side of the backcourt. His twenty-four-foot (7.3m) jump shot gave the Bulls the win. "That was just instinct," Paxson says. "You catch and you shoot. It's something I've done hundreds of thousands of times in my life."

ABOVE: Duke's Christian Laettner made a habit of providing the Blue Devils with fantastic finishes. RIGHT: Indiana's Rik Smits capped a furious exchange of last-second shots and beat Orlando with this jumper in the 1995 NBA playoffs.

It's a little more complicated than that. Shooting a basketball can be a simple task when the player is alone on the court working on form. It gets to be more of a challenge when there is a defensive player working to stop the ball from finding the goal. When there is an entire game riding on one shot, the pressure can be excruciating. Some players love to encounter that circumstance.

First at the University of Cincinnati and now with the Los Angeles Lakers, guard Nick Van Exel has repeatedly rescued his team from difficult situations. In one 1995 NBA playoff game against the San Antonio Spurs, he made a last-second shot to send the game into overtime, and then another in overtime to win the game.

"I think about 60 percent is confidence, about 30 percent rhythm and everything, and the form has to be good, too," Van Exel says. "It all comes into play, but you've got to have the confidence. My confidence is at 100 percent all the time. I like pressure situations. I think I'm a pressure player. When the game is on the line, please give me the ball."

Former Los Angeles guard Jerry West, now the team's general manager and Van Exel's boss, made so many late-game shots he earned the nickname "Mr. Clutch," but none was quite like the sixty-footer (18.3m) he made to send the third game of the 1970 championship

series with the New York Knicks into overtime. Those on the court recalled West didn't heave the ball, he merely shot it. Dave DeBusschere, the New York Knicks forward who was standing closest to the basket as the ball went through, fainted when he saw what happened. The Knicks won the game and the series anyway.

Center Christian Laettner of Duke University is not only the leading scorer in the history of the NCAA Tournament, he is also one of its most heroic players. He twice made jump shots at the final buzzer to place the Blue Dev-

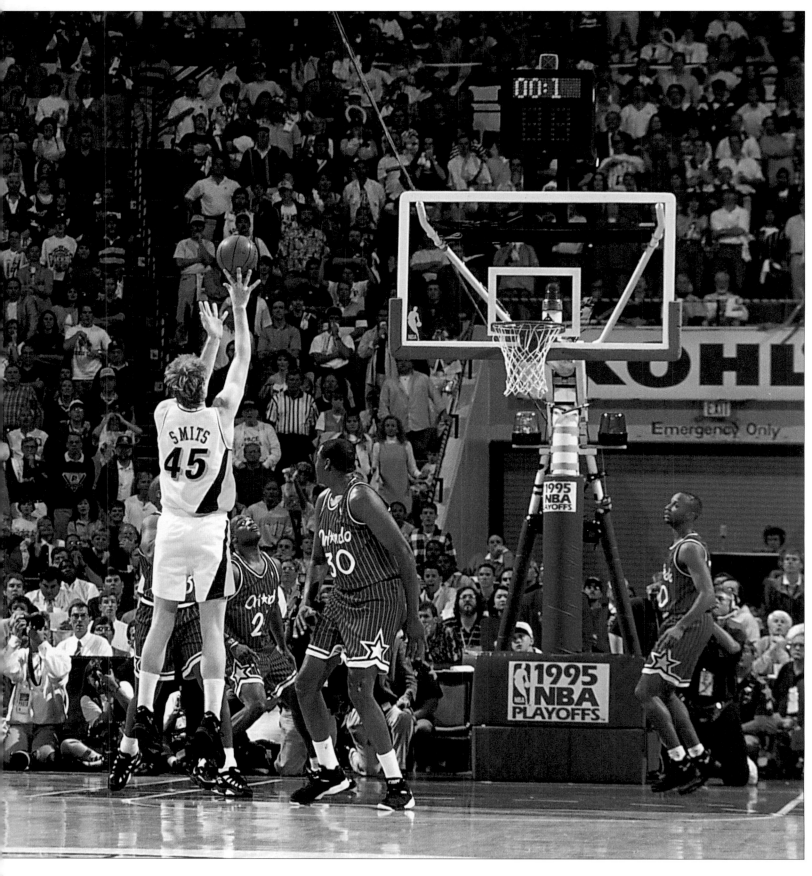

ils into the Final Four. The first knocked out Connecticut in the 1990 East Region championship, Laettner throwing an inbound pass, stepping across the sideline to receive the ball back, then dribbling and leaning in for a sixteen-foot (4.9m) jumper that gave Duke a 79–78 win in overtime. The next year, in 1991, Laettner made the 2 free throws that clinched Duke's NCAA semifinal win against top-ranked and unbeaten Nevada-Las Vegas.

In 1992, he topped all that with a spinning seventeen-footer (5.2m) to beat Kentucky 104–103 in overtime, after

Grant Hill threw a seventy-foot (20m) inbound pass to Laettner near the top of the key. All this happened in 2.1 seconds. "I can't believe it happened to me twice in a career," Laettner says. His shot provided a most suitable ending to the game many believe was the best college game ever played. "As a guy who loves the game for the game, you always hope you can be involved in something like this," Duke coach Mike Krzyzewski said afterward. "And I was."

BIBLIOGRAPHY

Carter, Craig, and Alex Sachere, eds. *The Sporting News Official NBA Guide*. St. Louis: The Sporting News Publishing Company, 1995.

Douchant, Mike. *Encyclopedia of College Basketball*. Detroit: Visible Ink Press, 1995.

Fox, Larry. *Illustrated History of Basketball*. New York: Grosset & Dunlap, 1974.

Hollander, Zander. *The NBA's Official Encyclopedia of Pro Basketball*. New York: NAL Books, 1981.

Hollander, Zander, and Alex Sachere. *The Official NBA Basketball Encyclopedia*. New York: Villard Books, 1989.

Isaacs, Neil D. *All the Moves: A History of College Basketball*. Philadelphia: J.B. Lippincott Company, 1975.

National Collegiate Athletic Association Staff. *Official NCAA Final Four Records Book*. Overland Park, Kans.: The National Collegiate Athletic Association, 1995.

Pluto, Terry. *Loose Balls: The Short, Wild Life of the American Basketball Association — As Told by the Players, Coaches, and Movers and Shakers Who Made It Happen*. New York: Simon & Schuster, 1991.

Puro, George, Alex Sachere, and Kyle Veltrop, eds. *The Sporting News Official NBA Register*. St. Louis: The Sporting News Publishing Company, 1995.

Savage, Jim. *The Encyclopedia of the NCAA Basketball Tournament*. New York: Dell Publishing Group, 1990.

Shaughnessy, Dan. *Seeing Red*. New York: Crown Publishers, 1994.

PHOTOGRAPHY CREDITS

© **Allsport:** p. 145 top; Jonathan Daniel: p. 144; Brian Drake: p. 65; Steven Dunn: pp. 21, 148 top; Tom Ewart: p. 167; Jim Gund: pp. 164, 165; Rick Stewart: p. 162

© **AP/Wide World Photos:** pp. 16 left, 19, 22, 23 top, 25, 35, 103, 129 inset, 131, 136 top, 147, 149 both, 160 right, 163, 168 left

© **Focus on Sport:** pp. 7, 20–21, 24 right, 26–27, 48 right, 66, 72, 96, 97 bottom, 98, 138–139, 166

© **National Basketball Hall of Fame:** p. 13 bottom

© **NBA Photo Library:** pp. 53 top, 58, 91

© **NBA Photos:** Victor Baldizon: p. 9; Bill Baptist: p. 85 top; Andrew D. Bernstein: pp. 2, 10, 36–37, 42, 44–45, 57, 61 inset, 80–81, 83, 88 right, 89, 99, 107 right, 130, 132 left, 135 top, 136 bottom, 151 left, 153, 154 both, 159; Nathaniel S. Butler: pp. 11, 12, 30, 39, 40, 50, 56, 70, 74, 78, 79, 85 bottom, 94, 100 right, 101, 109, 115, 124, 128, 132 right, 134, 155, 158, 161, 169; Lou Capozzola: pp. 63, 133; Jim Cummings: p. 92; Scott Cunningham: pp. 59, 73, 93 left, 95, 114, 157 left; Sam Forencich: pp. 43 right, 68, 80 inset, 111 bottom; Barry Gossage: pp. 6, 29, 43 left,

51, 67, 84, 97 top, 102, 104–105, 106; Don Grayston: pp. 41, 77; Andy Hayt: pp. 8, 54–55, 87 top, 100 left, 152, 156; Richard Lewis: pp. 60, 112; Fernando Medina: pp. 38, 90; Al Messerschmidt: p. 125 top; Betsy Peabody Rowe: p. 52; Jeff Reinking: p. 157 right; Jon Soohoo: p. 93 bottom; Noren Trotman: pp. 69 top, 75 top inset; Scott Wachter: p. 69 bottom

© **Rich Clarkson and Associates:** pp. 82 both, 108, 110, 113, 116 bottom, 118–119 both, 121, 127, 141 both, 145 bottom, 146, 148 bottom, 150 top, 161 left

© **Bob Rosato:** pp. 34, 45 inset, 104 left

© **Sportschrome:** p. 64

© **Spurlock Photography:** Michael Hebert: pp. 46, 53 bottom, 71, 75 bottom inset, 117; Brian Spurlock: pp. 17, 49, 76, 86, 87 right, 88 left, 107 left, 111 top, 116 top, 122–123 both, 125 bottom inset, 126, 151 right

© **UPI/Corbis-Bettmann:** pp. 13 bottom, 14 both, 15, 16 right, 18 inset, 23 bottom, 24 left, 28, 31, 32–33, 36, 47 both, 48 left, 120, 135 bottom inset, 137, 140, 142–143 both, 150 bottom, 160 left, 165 top

INDEX